sham
a beginner's guide

TERESA MOOREY

A catalogue record for this title is available from the British Library

ISBN 0 340 68010 5

First published 1997
Impression number 10 9 8 7 6 5 4 3 2
Year   2000 1999 1998 1997

Typeset by Transet Limited, Coventry, England
Printed in Great Britain for Hodder & Stoughton, a division of Hodder Headline plc,
338 Euston Road, London NW1 3BH by Cox and Wyman Limited, Reading.

CONTENTS

Chapter 4 Shamanic cosmology 49

Chapter 5 Totem animals and power animals 68

Chapter 6 Tools, crafts and practices 95

Dedication

To all the members of Rainbow Lodge, and to everyone at Different Drum. Thank you for sharing your experiences, your feelings and your knowledge so openly, which has been so helpful to me. Especially, thanks to Carolyn and Jan for organising the Lodge and the group with such commitment and wisdom. Blessings.

Acknowledgements

Thanks to Carolyn Finlay for reading through the manuscript, and for being constructive and encouraging.

Many thanks to Kenneth Meadows for corresponding with me and for so kindly supplying me with written and recorded material.

Thanks also to Leo Rutherford for sending me information.

Thanks, as always, to Sean Knight of the Church of All Worlds in Australia, for helping me keep the Southern Hemisphere perspective in mind.

INTRODUCTION

You are not enclosed within your bodies, nor confined to houses or fields.
That which is you dwells above the mountain and roves with the wind.

Kahlil Gibran, The Prophet

Many of us are finding that the need to reclaim the sacred is becoming more and more pressing in our daily lives. Not only do we see the undeniable damage that our way of life is inflicting on the ecosystem, we also observe that internally we have dried up – become desouled, uninspired, deprived of meaning. Many of us are stranded in the dust-bowls of the spirit, while we pursue material goals that seem increasingly devoid of true value. Conventional religion may offer little promise to those seeking direct experience of the transcendent, wishing to unite body and spirit in a feeling of wholeness and in vibrant celebration and honour of all that is Life.

Shamanic practices open pathways to the sublime in all of us, and foster a deep and loving respect for all that lives, through stones, crystals, trees, plants, animals and humans themselves. To the shaman, all is alive, all is sacred and all is connected in a cosmic web of beauty and 'beingness'. The ways of the shaman are both earthy and ethereal, for the Divine exists in everything we see, hear and touch, and consciousness can be expanded by direct experience of multilevel reality, in shamanic journeying. The shaman lives by experience, and in respect and wonderment – she or he is not bound by doctrine. And the shaman does not have to believe, for the shaman knows.

1

Individuals and groups are currently evolving shamanic practices that have links with and are inspired by native traditions, notably those of the native Americans. However, we cannot really hope to imitate these ways, nor is it right that we should, for our needs and potentials are different. Yet we can learn, borrow and be inspired in an attitude of respect. We can and should also evolve our own shamanism, drawing on the forgotten traditions of our culture and seeking inspiration regarding the ways we need to develop. Shamanism is about healing, and meeting needs that are relevant to us today.

This book is intended as a basic introduction to the contemporary seeker, defining and beginning to explore shamanic experience in a modern context, establishing understanding, a point of view and hopefully contacts with like-minded souls. References are made to native American and Celtic mythology, but there are other mythologies, other traditions – there is no right way. What is important is to find a way that works, that is inspiring, unifying and relevant to us today.

The way of the shaman is a path of truth. Find your own truth and respect the truths of others. Walk in beauty. Good journey!

Teresa Moorey
Beltane 1996

CHAPTER 1

WHAT IS SHAMANISM?

*He said . . . that everything is alive and singing its own
song and that we, the two-leggeds are our own chants.
He was asking me to be present and in each moment.*

Joseph Rael, *Beautiful Painted Arrow*

Shamanism is the most ancient spiritual practice of all. It entails
no dogma, and very few rules, for shamanism is about doing,
experiencing and knowing. It is a path of the heart – the heart that
opens and enfolds all of the natural world. It is a way of beauty and
balance. The shaman has direct participation in realms of
experience other than physical reality, and she or he makes use of
these encounters, for shamanism is an active pursuit. Although the
worlds travelled by the shaman are not the same as our day-to-day

3

reality, they are nevertheless real. To the shaman reality has many levels, only one of which is revealed by our ordinary senses. Experience of these levels is accessible to most of us, not just a select few. We just have to learn to open our inner eyes.

All cultures doubtless have a shamanic heritage, rooted back in time before time, when human consciousness still merged, to some extent, with plant and animal, with the energies of the earth and the cosmos itself. Indeed, all religions have a shamanic thread, a mystical undercurrent, which is, arguably, the essence of religious truth. In a sense shamanism is 'active mysticism'. The shamanic trance is different from that of the medium, the Delphic oracle of the ancient world, or the modern practice of channelling, for the role of the shaman involves conscious use of the trance state for a purpose. Today, when we are threatened by global disaster as a result of our manipulative contempt for the Earth, when our wells of belief have run dry and our old catechisms are meaningless, the way of the shaman shows us how we may hope to find validity again, both within us and without.

Relevance in the past and today

When we first hear the word 'shaman' it may conjure for us images of a capering medicine man, dressed in feathers and skins, staring through wild tresses with the eyes of a madman, perhaps enduring unbelievable pain and ordeal to attain transcendent experience. This can be confusing to the contemporary seeker, or it may be hypnotic. We may wonder what we can possibly have in common with the tribesman, or we may fall into an empty imitation, trying to recapture we know not quite what. We are rather like uprooted trees, roots questing in the dry air for our mother soil.

In a way, shamanism is about finding our way back to this soil, which is the seed-bed of the soul. It is about recalling and reclaiming the oneness that we share with creation, while retaining

our separateness also. Our minds work differently from our ancestors' minds and our immediate needs are different, for instance we do not need help with hunting and day-to-day survival. We do not have the stamina or the skills to live close to nature. However, this certainly does not mean that shamanism has slender relevance. It has everything for us. It is the quintessence of what so many of us seek today, in semis, mansions, high-rises and travellers' vans, and yes, it is still concerned with survival, only now it isn't a question of getting enough meat or having enough animal skins to see us through a hard winter. It is a matter of the survival of the planet herself, which we can only achieve by absorbing, at a profound level, how much, how very much we are a part of her.

What is a shaman?

Shamans are women and men who are spiritually alive, and who experience different levels of existence from everyday reality. Shamans learn to work with cosmic forces, and the forces of nature which are in us and around us. They appreciate that all that exists lives, and is furthermore interconnected and interdependent – strands woven on a cosmic loom. Mute rocks, babbling streams, clouds, trees, birds, fish, animals and people all have a life, all are different frequencies in the spectrum of 'beingness'. This belief that all lives has been called 'animism' and dismissed as rudimentary. However, in many ways it is the summit of spirituality.

A shaman can be male or female, and in this book I shall be referring to the shaman as 'he' or 'she' at different times. The female shaman is sometimes called a 'shamanka'. There is a suggestion that the first shamans were female, in the time when the ways of the instinctual feminine were held in reverence. In the more recent history of many cultures, shamanism seems to have become more a male province. Certainly today it is a pursuit that is equally open to both sexes. A true definition of a 'shaman' is elusive, for the shaman exists in her actions, and it is more helpful to think of shamanism as something one does, rather than 'being' a shaman – it is much more a dynamic function than a precisely defined role.

You may be feeling attracted to shamanic ways, but fear it may be beyond you in some fashion. However, if you love life, if you feel certain that much exists that is outside the realm of ordinary experience, and if you dream, then you have the keys to the doors of shamanic perception, and you can learn how to open them.

Belief and Knowing

Shamanic 'knowing' is very different from religious 'belief'. Belief requires a conscious decision, an 'act of faith', and the internal stress that results from deciding to believe something when you do not 'know' it often gives rise to conflict. This has been seen to occur in ways small and large, for in the case of belief there is often the impulse to wipe out inner doubt by convincing as many other people as possible that we are 'right'. Nonetheless, however many people are won over to the point of view, the vestiges of doubt still remain, and there the seeds are sown of much conflict. Wars are fought over beliefs, but inner knowledge brings a sense of peace. True shamanic experience brings inner balance, integrity, joy and fulfilment.

Our Legacy of Duality

Logic and linear thinking are greatly prized in our culture, and indeed the benefits of science are unarguable. However, its drawbacks are also all too evident. The perils of the hole in the ozone layer, over-population, the tragedy of deforestation and pollution – all these are well known. What is less recognised is how cramped, how toxic and lifeless is the mental space we inhabit.

The compartmentalised mind needs everything to be neatly arranged into clearly defined sections that often resolve into opposites – good/bad, right/wrong, light/dark, man/woman – and many experiences, entities, beliefs tend to be filed in one section or the other. This has resulted in a huge amount of richly valuable and beautiful material

being denigrated, disregarded or denied. For instance, the feminine has been packaged together with darkness, intuition, body, matter, instinct and regarded with all the suspicion of a ticking carrier bag in a subway. Ambiguity, intuition, dreams, inconsistencies – all these are anathema to logic. Unfortunately, in throwing our instincts on the bonfire along with all the other 'undesirables' we have forgotten how to be part of and how to be true caretakers of the exquisite and finely-tuned planet that is our Mother.

The ego, too, loves black and white, the 'me' and the 'not me'. Threatened by shipwreck on the stormy waters of the Unconscious, the ego bales out anything suspect, anything not quite 'rational'. Uneasy, guilty, under siege, our conscious minds are all too apt to deny anything within us that we, or the society we inhabit, might censure. Unerringly these despised traits surface as things we condemn in other people – we are all familiar with the driver who snarls at others for his own mistakes, the rapist or murderer who blames his or her victim, the fanatic who kills in the name of 'ethnic cleansing'. All these are unwilling and unable to face the glorious untidiness of their own humanity. Very occasionally a person may kill rather than face it, for it may be easier to hunt down an enemy than to face one's inner conflicts. Things are easier when they are split – 'I' can be good if 'you' are bad. All is simple, comfortable, and we all know who the good guys are and who are the bad guys.

The separation of God and matter

One of the saddest splits, and possibly the grandfather of all other splits, is one we have struggled with since the relative peace of the Bronze Age gave way to Iron Age strife – the split between God and Matter, Created and Creator. In earlier times God – who was rather seen as Goddess – dwelt *within* creation, and each daily act, each common thing participated in the divine totality. As the human ego grew, seeking a safe sense of separation from the instinctual, so God

became masculinised, intellectualised and external to the material world. Laws were devised to keep the primal in check. The flaming sword of the intellect barred passage to Eden. This was a necessary phase, no doubt, but perhaps now it is a phase we need to progress from.

As a result of this the Earth has been treated as something unholy, to be exploited, harnessed and overcome. Divine spirit, that breathed in the wind, that sang in the waterfall, that leapt in each sprouting seed and scuttling, leaping, flying creature was withdrawn to be the province of a priesthood – and the word 'priesthood' is significant. The old priestesses with their lore of earth wisdom and knowledge of the Goddess were superseded. Rigid laws controlled a human spirit that was no longer trusted. So religions were born that vaunted 'spirituality' while discouraging the practice of it as 'forbidden arts' that despise the earth and the body and yet encourage rampant materialism by denying direct access to the Divine.

And so the human mind took up voluntary, tragic residence in a cell of its own devising. The walls are fear and ignorance, the wardens are all the 'thou shalts' and 'thou shalt nots' by which our questing spirits are caged. And the key? The direct shamanic experience is certainly one key, part of the ancient inheritance of mankind, abode of a wisdom that transcends logic, day-to-day consciousness and that certainly transcends dualism and calcified laws. Shamanic participation reveals the essential unity in all creation. The key to this is simply lying around, hardly rusted with age, waiting for us to open our inner eyes, to pick it up and swing wide the doors of perception. Merely by acknowledging that this key exists brings us to the brink of finding it. From there it is a relatively short step to expanding awareness.

The shamanic experience

There are two main aspects to shamanism. One is the recognition that all is divine. This is more than a respect for nature – more even than a love for it. It is much more than obeying an injunction that

you must prize all you see as a gift of God. In shamanism there are no such injunctions, because there is no need for them. The shaman simply perceives all as divine – feels it as divine. Nature is not a gift of God, it *is* God, and of course it is Goddess, too. The shaman sees with the eye of the mystic. She is one with the Stone People, the Cloud Spirits, her being is dissolved in a solution of wonderment that stirs together the sun, moon and stars, each atom of air and each particle of granite in a suffusion of joy – of ecstasy.

If this sounds somewhat inaccessible, remember that there are stages in this process. We can start with glimpses, we can walk with our doubts until we can walk our talk, dance our dreams. It is okay to stumble, to be unsure, to find vivid experience of the all-pervasive Divine extremely elusive. If you are attracted to the shamanic path, if you have taken just the very first wavering step along it then you have had a glimpse, however fleeting, however indistinct – and that glimpse is enough for now.

The second aspect to shamanism is the shamanic journey. It is in such journeys that we begin to experience multilevelled reality, to know that we exist in many dimensions and to explore these dimensions, to uncover the shaman within.

The shamanic journey

The simplest way to describe the shamanic journey is that it is like a waking dream. This is a lucid dream – you know you are dreaming. You, as shaman, are in control – not of all that happens in your journey, for, as you will quickly discover, the realms you travel in have their own life and their own laws. But you are in control of how you react to what happens. And you are also in control of beginning and ending the experience when you wish.

Shamanic journeying is in some ways akin to guided visualisation, with which you may be familiar. Guided visualisation is like being taken on a tour, in a bus. The windows are sealed, so you cannot smell the scents, breathe the air. Your view is restricted to a narrow

window, through which you can see only indistinctly, and the courier perpetually distracts you by giving a running commentary about the landscape, the flora and fauna and even gives you suggestions about how you may react to what you see. Not a very immediate experience!

In contrast, when taking a shamanic journey, you are in the driver's seat. Far more than this, even. You are a bird that flies over panoramas of billowing hills, you are a wolf that sniffs and snarls as an orchestra of scents choreographs the beating of your heart. Or you are an otter, or a dolphin in the laughing embrace of water. Simply you may be your own heroic 'self' finding entrances to the Otherworld in caves and tree boles, encountering beings of wonderment, wisdom – sometimes puzzling, sometimes scary. At the end of your journey it is you, in company possibly with like-minded journeyers, who will explore what it all may mean.

Perhaps the most important point to remember about the shamanic journey is that it always has a purpose. At first your purpose is likely to be fairly simple, such as locating your totem or power animal. Later on you may journey for specific answers to all manner of questions from your money management, through relationships and on to the most abstract questions regarding your spiritual development. Further than this, the advanced shaman journeys to effect soul-healing for those who need it, although this is outside the scope of this book. It could be said, however, that all shamanic journeys are healing, not only for he who journeys but also to the planet. For each time a journey is undertaken, each time the paths between the worlds are trodden, the way becomes clearer for others who follow and connection between this world and the Otherworlds is strengthened. So wisdom and new energy can find their way into our wearied realms.

Making a shamanic journey involves relaxing deeply, in a dim light, closing your eyes and watching what takes place with your inner sight, having identified the purpose of your journey. You may walk, glide, fly, creep. You may have physical sensations, perhaps quite sexual. You will feel, see, hear and experience many things. Usually you are aided by the beat of a drum. On some journeys very little

happens. You get distracted, you don't feel 'there', it's fragmentary, even silly and you may dismiss it all as 'just imagination'. Perhaps, if this is your first journey, nothing happens at all. We shall be looking more closely at the journey in our final chapter. Rest assured that if you truly wish to journey it is extremely likely that you will be able to.

What makes a good shaman?

Traditionally shamanism was not usually sought as a vocation. It entailed much responsibility to the tribe and its members and was an arduous and demanding practice. Usually the shaman would find himself chosen, either through a severe trauma, an episode of madness, or a Near Death Experience – or possibly by all three! Indeed the shaman was – and is – a wounded healer, and sometimes the practice of shamanism was the only way to make sense of a riven world.

These days initiatory experience is not nearly so drastic – and yet all is relative. We no longer face the perils of our forbears – our challenges are different, but no less threatening. Many of us face loss of soul in the demands of modern living. Emotional crises rip us apart and we are called upon to look within ourselves and make radical changes in a way that people living close to nature are not likely to have to do. If you wish to pursue shamanism it is probable that you have suffered at least one substantial crisis in your life, something that wrenched you around, caused you to look at life from a totally different perspective, swept away the parameters of your security and made you feel that a part of you had indeed died. Probably you carry your own soul-wounds, and these wounds can be openings to other levels of reality and passages for healing energy to pass through.

Like anything else, shamanism has stages. Not everyone who embarks on a shamanic path will develop as a soul-healer, or as a poet, seer, teacher or story-teller. However, a 'good' shaman is effectual. This effectuality extends from the fact that the journey always has a purpose. However, it is more far-reaching and also more mundane.

Although the shaman walks between the worlds, a creature of the twilight wilds, he is neither 'spaced out' nor a 'drop out'. The shaman's feet have to be planted firmly on the good soil of Mother Earth before he can journey effectively. Shamans have to cope reasonably soundly with the demands of everyday life – work, family, commitments, routines. Having grasped these matters firmly the decision can then be taken to give up some involvements in order to give more time to shamanic ways – but this is not intended as a cop out for those who can't be bothered to deal with everyday life, who prefer to believe they are too 'spiritual', who cannot concentrate, who are looking for an escape, who never feel truly 'here'. The truth is if a person cannot manage to be fully present in his physical body when necessary, then he is unlikely to be able to be properly present in his soul-body when he journeys. Much of this book will be devoted to grounding and orientation, giving a philosophical and practical background in preparation for the journey. It is important to engage with life before engaging as a shaman. Furthermore, a shaman needs humour, common sense and an open mind. All these may be more valuable than a propensity to daydream.

Modern shamanism

Indigenous people, such as the Australian Aborigines, the Siberian Evenks, and, most notably, the American Indians all have a living shamanic culture that is greatly envied by many contemporary seekers. Later on we shall be mentioning one or two of the native American ways, for these are of great interest, and have been the basis of much inspiration. Kenneth Meadows (*The Medicine Way* – see 'Further Reading') says, of the Indian tradition

> *Until recent years that knowledge and wisdom appeared to have been lost. It was, however, being guarded and protected, and now it can be made available ... to the genuine seeker. For the time has arrived ... for a revival of the ancient wisdom ... this constructive way is not to be limited to a particular race, creed, nation or group, but [to] be generally accessible ...*

It seems that the intention of the native American Elders may have been to make available their store of wisdom, at a later date, to those who sought in a time of the world's great need. It seems that time is now upon us.

However, to believe that we can deeply grasp the nature of native American ideas may be presumptuous. Representatives of these cultures seem to live perpetually conscious of multilevel reality. Their lives are a metaphor of Spirit, and this is conveyed in their language. This is explored by Joseph Rael in *Beautiful Painted Arrow* which you can find listed in 'Further Reading'. It is a most poignant realisation that no Redman, of this graceful and awakened race, is represented in the highest councils of the world – that fact seems to epitomise all that is Philistine about our race. Nonetheless, it is also important that we seek to recapture the spirit of our own culture – for instance that of the Celts. We need to find a shamanism that is relevant to who we are and where we are today – and that honours our ancestry and the spirit of the land that nourishes us.

Much shamanism is practised in groups and lodges, and it can be very helpful to be part of a supportive circle of people who are pursuing similar goals. In such settings there is usually an experienced leader who encourages the group, organises the work and themes for journeying and presides over general discussions where experiences of journeys may be shared. In lodges a certain amount of commitment and experience is likely to be possessed by all members, but in more open groups, workshops and courses – of which there are many – all sorts of people may attend, from the complete beginner to the much more advanced.

If you wish to pursue shamanism there is a lot to be said for having some support and the opportunity to benefit from the experience of others. However, if you wish to work alone there is no reason why you should not. Drumming tapes (we shall see later how important the sound of the drum is for shamanic journeying) can be readily obtained. However, it is important to prepare yourself well in terms of philosophical framework before you begin, and to follow sensible rules.

Not a 'new age' diversion

The pursuit of shamanism is serious. It is not a hobby or a pastime, it is not for dabblers, ego-trippers, those who seek a quick high, an escape or an aura of the exotic. It is enjoyable, yes – and there is often humour, but there is also a sense of responsibility.

Physical journeys are not without hazards. We all know we must drive carefully if we are to reach our destination intact, and that we need maps in uncharted territory. A shamanic journey is many times safer than a trip down the average motorway, but it should nonetheless be treated with respect. Here we are pushing back the boundaries of our consciousness, and that is a considerable undertaking. So prepare for shamanic experience by some honest introspection and some study. Even if you decide to work alone ensure that you have a support system if you need it – someone to talk to about your journey experiences. Most of us struggle still, at some level with vestiges of guilt, dualism and much family baggage. This can surface in surprising ways as we progress deeper – for it is true that in many ways you will meet yourself on your journeys.

One of the important aspects of shamanic practice may be to achieve some understanding of death and its meaning and perhaps to know how to die, when the time comes.

Masters of ecstasy

The shaman is a master of ecstasy. Usually we understand ecstasy as total, all-enveloping joy of mind and body, and indeed that is the case. For a better understanding it is useful to consider the construction of the word. Ecstasy means 'ex-stasis' – going out of the static, out of the body, of the normal, hidebound way of being. This can be achieved by journeying, but there are other, less clearly defined approaches which may also be remembered.

Some rock musicians are modern 'masters of ecstasy' by virtue of the state of mind they generate and the power of the music. Rock

has been called 'mindless' but usually the only 'mind' that it lacks is the robotic, restrictive plodding that we usually think of as awareness. Many (but not all) rock musicians have a message that is certainly about pushing back the frontiers of the way we look at life, and some of it is deeply philosophical. A good rock concert certainly lifts us out of ourselves, leaves us washed clean, shining with delight, vibrating with energy. Rock music, at its best, mythologises the daily life that is familiar to us all. Suddenly there are angels on the pavement, heroes in shop doorways. The beat of the drum is the heartbeat of the gods and we move to it – we dance our dream and all dances with us, everything is alive. We lose ourselves, we get 'out of our heads' and we feel larger, we feel great, we feel that all has colour and meaning.

Shamanism, as we have seen, is active, and true dance is unity, purpose and beauty. These concepts are further explored by the urban shaman Gabrielle Roth in *Maps to Ecstasy* listed in 'Further Reading'. This is an important alternative dimension which we can remember, although this book concentrates on a different approach. If you prefer other types of music to rock, these may well provide pathways to ecstatic experience. The particular advantage of rock music is the drumbeat, however, with which mind, body, spirit and emotions resonate.

This sounds quite different from inner journeys that are usually undertaken when our bodies are still and quiet. However in both cases we are out of ourselves, out of our normal day-to-day consciousness. We may have to work at our journeying for it to reach the all-embracing power of sound as generated by the rock masters. And yet there is a vivid physicality and sexual dimension to journeying as you may discover when you begin to experience it. With journeying we direct the process, we control without constraining, we ride the beat like a skilful horseman who knows when to give the horse its head and ride like a madman, on the wings of the wind – and afterwards we evaluate and assimilate what we have encountered – we do not simply enjoy. But enjoyment is important, and we should not forget the importance of dance and movement.

practice

There are two areas of practice after our first chapter. The first concerns experience of the natural world, the second concerns self-knowledge. However, both of these are areas of ongoing exploration. Please use these exercises as a start, see how you react to them and devise your own to take you further. Give yourself times for quiet reflection – perhaps ten minutes a day – to meditate on a question concerning either of the subjects. Where are you being led? What do you need to experience? Where might you go and who might help you? What further work do you need to do? Make your explorations quietly and steadily. There is no need for haste, for this is a life task. Let yourself be excited and absorbed by it.

1 The tree people

Most of us interested in alternative ways of perceiving and loving nature are aware that trees have personality and power. They have an essence and an aura – indeed they are probably far more evolved as creatures along their special path than we are as humans. Native Americans call the trees the Standing People.

Go out into woodland and walk with this knowledge in your heart – walk with the spirits of the trees. Not all trees are friendly, for some are hurt and have treachery within them – a graphic description of wicked Old Man Willow and the encounter the Hobbits have with him is given in J.R.R. Tolkein's *Lord of the Rings*. However, most trees possess spirits of great loveliness and transcendent wisdom. Walk until you find a tree that seems to welcome you.

Go up to the trees – touch it, hug it, lean against it. Hopefully you have chosen somewhere private enough not to be bothered by the stares of others. Forget how you may look and just be with the tree. Close your eyes – what comes to mind? Do you feel this tree has something to say to you? Sit quietly under the tree for as long as you like and notice your surroundings. Take note of what happens –

the flight of birds, the fall of leaves, a rainbow, a raindrop. Try not to analyse for the moment.

After a while stand up and feel what it is like to *be* the tree. This is different from communing – this is partaking of the essence, a shamanic activity. Feel your feet turning into roots and snaking down into the soil. Is it soft and welcoming? Sweet, rich, thick, or dry and stony? Feel your branches reaching to the sky, kissed by the wind, tickled gently by the birds. You may like to hold up your arms for this, but remember, they may get tired. Your body is the trunk, covered by rough bark, tough, yet filled with the slow oozing of sap. Concentrate on being the tree, imagining all the details, then stop. Now you *are* the tree. Just be, for a while.

When you are ready come back to normal awareness. Now you may interpret what has happened, analyse it, wonder about it, dream about it. Keep a notebook for shamanic work, and be very sure to write everything down in it.

2 The GENOGRAM

The importance of self-knowledge is now so widely recognised that it has become a cliché and a modern obsession. Psycho-babble is heard everywhere – phrases whose meaning have been lost because the practice has been accepted without being understood and appreciated. We have packaged it and labelled it, and we may buy it, without quite knowing what we are doing.

However, true self-knowledge is the most noble pursuit there is, and without it no other knowledge is worth much. Self-knowledge is vital for us in shamanic work, because anything that we have not acknowledged will come between us and our shamanic experience. This is not to say that 'getting to know yourself' is a task that can ever be completed, but the necessity for self-knowledge is something we need to realise, humbly, however wise and experienced we are, and we can always know ourselves a bit better.

Self-knowledge is much more than realising that our mothers didn't love us enough or our fathers were full of hypocrisy, and the path to it can be very painful, bringing knowledge of emotions we have suppressed and unearthing much about us that may be quite revolting to us.

This exercise is just a very small beginning on this route. Begin it by telling yourself that you are lovable, whatever. All that you are and have been is acceptable to the cosmos. The air, the green grass, the moonlight – all will take you in their embrace, regardless of how you may judge yourself, or feel others judge you. Tell yourself you are 'okay' – feel it if you can. If not, tell yourself anyway. This is something you can repeat at any time in your life and work.

Now take a large piece of paper and draw your 'genogram'. This is really a family tree, done pictorially. Draw each of the family members as stick people – you don't have to be artistic. Use colours if you like. Surround your irritable auntie with some jagged red lines, draw your dad behind his newspaper. Allow your instincts to surface and draw them on paper, however crude you may feel your efforts are. Allow yourself to get absorbed in this task – improvise – draw lines between the characters to indicate relationships. Broken or wavy lines may indicate relationships that were/are tenuous or fractured, ribbons to indicate gentle bonds, thick lines for restrictions. Indicate people who have died or are/were in some way unavailable for you by ringing them or colouring them according to your feelings. Perhaps even though someone has passed on from this life you may feel their love is still available – or you may be angry with them. Give yourself time and scope. Put down what you feel as best you can.

When you have done all you can for the moment stop and examine your work. How does it look? Where do you fit in? When I first did this exercise I was amazed to see I had left myself out! There all my family was, each person in their various guises and patterns, all the characters of the play that was my early life, and yet I was missing! I had to think quite a lot about that, for it was significant to me.

You can continue to work on your genogram for weeks, months, years, re-doing and changing it as new realisations and feelings come to you and as you evolve. You can make a collage, using photos. You may represent certain important people symbolically, making a geometric pattern. You can use any medium for this work. If you like sculpting you may do this too, perhaps using clay that doesn't need firing, which is readily obtainable in art shops and large stationers. Finally you may make a shield. This was something that many native Americans did, although naturally our spirit and approach are different. The shield was not intended for physical protection. Rather it was a statement of power and identity, and so the 'protection' it gave was self-knowledge. You can make a family shield, using animal skin, canvas, embroidery frame or whatever. The circle is usually considered to be the ideal shape, but other shapes may feel more appropriate, such as an oval or diamond. Make your shield as small or large as you like and place on it a representation of your ancestry, your place in your own human tree and the inner legacy you have. You can include difficult things, of course, but try to ensure that you have identified some strengths they have given you. We shall be looking at shieldmaking in more detail later on.

If and when you make your shield you may feel that you have completed something. You have – you have completed a stage, a circuit of the spiral. The exploration doesn't end here. Later you may wish to make another shield, do other work. Congratulate yourself on what you have done, feel a sense of achievement, and tell yourself you will continue on your fascinating quest.

SOURCES AND BACKGROUND

Woman like the big eagle am I
Woman like the opossum am I
Woman who examines am I
Woman like the hunting dog am I
And woman like the wolf am I

Shamanic chant uttered by Maria Sabina, Mazatec shaman

The strong bull of the earth, the horse of the steppe,
The strong bull has bellowed!
The horse of the steppe has trembled!
I am above you all, I am a man!
I am the man who has all gifts!
I am the man created by the Lord of Infinity...

Chant of Yakut shaman

The practice of shamanism is found all over the globe, in Siberia, Lapland, North and South America, Australia, Indonesia, Tibet, China and Japan. It could be said that there are shamanic threads in all cultures, and it has been suggested that shamanism was once practised universally. Mircea Eliade (see 'Further Reading') writes: '... we would consider it fundamental in the human condition, and hence known to the whole of archaic humanity'. The shaman may be also a mystic, poet, magician and priest. In societies where shamanism is practised, the shaman does not necessarily hold the monopoly on religious life, for some aspects may be carried out by an officiating priest, for example. The shaman is called upon for specific purposes that involve journeys of the soul, such as healing.

Eliade, acknowledged authority on the subject, defines shamanism as 'technique of ecstasy'. However, not every ecstatic is a shaman, nor is every magician or priest. Eliade states 'the shaman specialises in a trance during which his soul is believed to leave his body and ascend to the sky or descend to the underworld'. Shamanism in the strictest sense is principally a phenomenon arising in Siberia and neighbouring areas, and the word derives from the Tungusic word *saman*. However, another source given by Joan Halifax – see 'Further Reading' – is the Vedic *sram*, which means 'to heat oneself or practise austerities' (*saman* may in fact be derived from *sram*). This latter derivation accords with accounts of shamans becoming very hot, being able to produce heat at will, eating live coals, walking on fire and undergoing terrible initiatory ordeals. However, a final definition of shamanism is elusive, and all the more so because it is an evolving practice. Many tribal traditions are almost irrelevant to us today, and yet there is also common ground.

Shamanic Initiation

This generally occurred through dreams, visions and trances, where the spirits 'elected' a new shaman by making themselves known to him. Often there was a crisis or life-threatening illness. The shamanic faculty may also be passed down through the bloodline,

or it may come as a result of a vision-quest, undertaken at puberty. The shaman takes a 'spirit flight' that would seem symbolically to heal the ancient rift between mankind and the sacred. He also faces horrifying underworld journeys to the sources of disease, and these journeys display similar features to many mythic tales, such as those of Odin, Orpheus in the Underworld, the descent of Inanna and many others.

Often the shaman is dismembered, in his vision, and may be boiled in a pot until only his bones remain. Then he is reassembled, bone by bone. Bone represents the very source of life and the most enduring part of the physical body. It symbolises both the transience of life – if we contemplate being reduced to a skeleton we are facing the reality of our death – and also the force of regeneration. It was important to the ancients that ancestral bones were preserved, often returned to 'wombs' of earth to await rebirth, and yet, although it is not literally the bones themselves that rise up, newly clad with flesh, bone is the basis of life. It is also said that bone is closest to spirit. Thus if we break a bone this may be a strong indication of a rupture in the soul life, or a spiritual change.

In the case of the Meso-American shaman, Ramon Medina Silva, the visionary dreams were followed by a snakebite that left him paralysed for six months. His grandfather, himself a shaman, saved the boy's life, telling him that he would one day be a great shaman. In many cases sickness precedes shamanic election. However, this certainly does not mean that the shaman is weak or ill, for the reverse is usually the case, with shamans being capable of withstanding tremendous ordeals and having superhuman stamina. Neither are shamans generally neurotic nor 'abnormal' in any way – in fact they usually display great energy and self-control, having healed themselves in the process of becoming a shaman.

After election the novice shaman is usually trained by a more experienced practitioner and may then have to undergo ordeals that would kill an ordinary person many times over. For instance, the Eskimo shaman Igjugarjuk, was towed on a sledge, in the depth of winter, far away from his dwelling and left for the space of a moon in a snow hut, completely alone, many miles from his village and without food or warm covering. After five days he was brought tepid

water, and again after fifteen days. He could not lie down, and was unable to move. After thirty days a helping spirit came to him in the guise of a beautiful woman, and he knew that he would acquire shamanic powers. Later he initiated his sister-in-law by hanging her on some tent poles in the snow and leaving her for five days, in midwinter blizzards. After this ordeal, during which she felt no cold, being protected by the spirits, Igjugarjuk shot her through the heart with a stone – the choice of stone, as opposed to bullet, meant she would retain connection with the earth – and she fell unconscious, but revived the following morning.

Such exploits, verified by anthropologists, attest to the powers of the human spirit that go far beyond what we might call 'normal'. People who have been less influenced by 'civilisation' may have access to inner resources with which we have lost contact, due to our insistence on the rational. However, it would be a dangerous mistake for anyone from the Western world to undertake such ordeals in the quest for shamanic revelation, for we are not equipped for these experiences and need to seek powers of soul-flight in less drastic ways.

Cosmology

Here the most prevalent theme is that of the three worlds: upper, middle and lower. We shall be looking at these in a modern context in a later chapter. At the centre of the three worlds is the World Tree, or axis mundi. However, this may also be seen as a Tree of Life, symbolic of nourishment, birth, rebirth and the cycle of life, as well as the planes of existence and levels of manifestation. The Goldi, the Dolgan and the Tungus believe that the souls of children perch on the branches of the Tree, like birds, until the time they are to be born. The concept of flight linked to transcendence or Otherworld experience is prevalent. The Yakut believe the Tree grows in primal paradise where the first man was born, fed by the milk of a woman whose body half emerges from the tree-trunk. Some shamans are believed to make their drum-shell from wood fallen from this Cosmic Tree (we shall be exploring the meanings of the drum in a later chapter). Shamans often symbolically climb the World Tree during shamanic sessions.

It is not always a tree that stands at the centre. It may also be a mountain, a rock or sometimes a building. In the case of the Evenks, the three worlds are linked by the Clan River. The Ngadju Dyaks of Borneo do not have a concept of three worlds, but only two, with the world of humans being a crossover, an amalgamation of the two. Whatever system is used, the shamanic journey works.

Spirits inhabit the worlds, and the shaman has one or more as his helper. These may be minor deities, ancestral spirits or animal familiars. The shaman calls on these at will – he is not possessed by them. The guardian spirit can be an aspect of the shaman's own identity, and shamans have been reported as going forth in an animal form. This may be the origin of the belief in werewolves, which is still strong in South America.

Other cosmological motifs include rainbows, bridges, roads of the dead (all seen as routes to the Otherworld), initiatory obstacles and openings that are open only momentarily, such as a path between clashing rocks, through which the initiate must pass, and risk destruction. Such rocks are symbolic of the view of opposing opposites, which must be transcended – something which can only be accomplished in an instant, not by reflection and slow passage. The mystical numbers seven and nine are repeatedly found. This may be reflected in the number of heavens passed through by the shaman or in characteristics of the journey – for instance the Vogul believe that a stairway of seven stairs has to be scaled to reach the sky, while the Altaic shaman has to pass through seven underworld obstacles. There is no space to examine these themes in depth, but it is interesting to note that both seven and nine are linked, in mystical doctrines, with the Moon. Representing, as it does, instinctual knowledge, it is not surprising to find traces of lunar symbolism in shamanic – or indeed any – mythology.

Rituals

Ritual is an outer sign of inner change. Many shamanic rituals have been puzzling to anthropologists, whose approach may be very

literal, and because of this shamans have sometimes been regarded as theatrical tricksters. However, the shaman is enacting sacred reality which possesses intense inner meaning and is part of 'scene setting' for soul-flight. In addition, ritual may have the effect of producing a change in the consciousness of observers, so enhancing the ambience necessary for the inner journey.

By drumming, rattle-shaking and frenzied dancing a trance state may be brought about. Movements may imitate those of an animal – for instance in the dance of the Beast Gods, of the Zuni Pueblo. Animal skins may be worn and animal cries emitted, and sometimes these cries, during an indoor shamanic session, may appear to come from different corners of the room. The point of this is, in a fashion which is hard to describe without the experience having been undertaken, to become one with the animal, to feel how that animal feels, to see, hear, smell with animal senses and to take on the powers of the animal. In this way the shaman strengthens himself and widens his perception and capabilities.

Rituals are involved in initiation rites, where the ascent of the soul is often symbolically enacted. Eliade writes (see 'Further Reading') 'Among the Pomo [of North America] the ceremony for entrance into the secret societies lasts four days, one day being devoted entirely to the climbing of a tree-pole from twenty to thirty feet long and six inches in diameter ... future Siberian shamans climb trees during or before their consecration ... the Vedic sacrificer also climbs a ritual post to reach heaven and the gods. Ascent by a tree, a liana or a rope is an extremely widespread mythical motif ...'. Again, the ritual enactment signifies an inner reality.

Shamans also have ritual costumes, perhaps made of feathers – the feather is a frequent, obvious symbol of flight – or animal skins. Donning the costume is a sign of the presence of the sacred, and in addition cosmology and metaphysical journey are often symbolically depicted upon the garment. The costume of a Yakut shaman may have between thirty and fifty pounds of metal ornaments attached, representing bones, female breasts and internal organs together with bird and animal shapes and a small figure of a canoe, with a man in it. The canoe is a frequent vehicle for flights of the soul. Masks and

caps are also often donned, and the shaman's drum may be decorated in a variety of ways. Tungus' drums may be ornamented with birds, snakes and animals, while some drums of Eastern Siberia bear no design. The selection of the wood for the drum is also important, and spirits will often tell the shaman where to find the correct tree. Afterwards a sacrifice may be made to the tree, for supplying the wood, for in this way the shaman shows his gratitude to the powers of Life and his acknowledgement that what he was is not his by 'right' but belongs to the cosmos and the tribe. The drum is most important as it represents the means by which the shaman makes his breakthrough into other levels of reality, and so the symbolism of the World Tree is often incorporated into the making of the drum.

Song too is a vital ingredient in shamanic activity. Song and music convey spiritual essence – an idea enshrined in the Medieval concept of the 'music of the spheres'. Singing is also a creative act, and a beautiful example of this is provided by the Australian Aborigines. Nevill Drury (see 'Further Reading') tells us the Aborigines:

> ... believe that the songs they continue to sing today are the same as those sung by their ancestors in the Dreamtime, when the gods brought the world into being. The most sacred songs are chanted at the special sites where the gods were thought to roam: these songs are considered to have a special magic which helps to produce abundant food and water supplies.

Song is also important to the bringing into the 'here and now' of shamanic experience, and sometimes on his return from a journey the shaman may break into a song that has been given to him by the spirits for the purpose of healing. Such songs are a precious part of the shaman's repertoire.

ÐRUGS

Drugs may be employed by shamans in various parts of the globe. Generally, a Siberian shaman who used drugs was regarded as

'second rate' but in other countries – notably Mexico and South America – entire cults are built around the use of certain sacred hallucinogenic plants, such as the psilocybe mushroom and the San Pedro cactus. These plants are used with supreme respect and venerated as being divine.

In cultures where hallucinogenic substances are ingested ceremonially there is a pervading attitude of reverence and solemnity. Dosage is carefully calculated by a shamanic Adept and the reactions and experiences of the initiate closely monitored. A psycho/spiritual framework is in place and time-honoured rituals exist to serve as containment for drug-induced visions and sensations. Even so, such experiences are often harrowing.

By contrast, in the West, drugs may be used recreationally and there are no readily accessible paradigms to give meaning and relevance to drug-induced experiences. Of course, there have been people who have used hallucinogens and believed they provoked a breakthrough in insight. For instance, Robin Skynner in *Life and How To Survive It* written with John Cleese (Mandarin, 1993) describes his experience of enlightenment as a result of research into LSD during psychiatric training;

> ... I had such massive blinkers on at that time that I doubt that I would ever have allowed myself to have a spiritual experience without a bit of 'chemical dynamite' ... So the drug ... encouraged me to take this side of life more seriously

Asked then by Cleese if he was tempted to take the drug again, Skynner replies

> No. For me it was like seeing a wonderful distant land from the top of a mountain. You knew that no matter how many more times you went up the mountain to look at it again, you still wouldn't get any closer to what you'd seen. To get to it you had to go back down and make your way along the ground, which I've been attempting to do ever since ...

The point here is that while in some places drugs may have been found to have a place, there is no doubt that taking them without proper safeguards can be highly dangerous, carrying risks of short-

or long-term damage to health. Taking drugs for 'fun' or just 'to see what happens' is totally at variance with shamanic goals, and no-one who is serious about wishing to follow this path (or who has a healthy respect for their body) would ever do so. Needless to say, drug-taking is also illegal. Most relevant of all to the pursuit of shamanism, drug-taking is quite unnecessary, and could possibly hinder the experience of transcendence. Shamanic experience can be sought and obtained by much safer, pleasanter and more reliable means, as this book is intended to show.

Psychology

The shamanic state, especially at its inception, has been likened to forms of mental illness, such as schizophrenia. There are several points in connection with this. First, while the shaman may begin her career in crisis, she certainly does not remain so, for the point of shamanism is controlled spirit-flight and effective use of transcendent states. Second, any 'dualistic' perception within the society, such as good/bad, spirit/matter, light/dark, which occurs in many cultures, is bound to provoke crisis in one whose mystical experiences go beyond this resolution into opposites, at once unifying them and rendering them meaningless. Third, our attitude to such illnesses as schizophrenia may just be misleading, for though these conditions entail an undeniably great degree of suffering, we totally fail to consider any possibility of the sacrality of these states or the possibility of spiritual revelation in connection with them – for instance, Mongolian lamas may advise the mentally unbalanced to become shamans. These are all points we may like to bear in mind.

Traditionally, shamans provided an invaluable function of making the territory of death accessible and the idea of death easier to face and integrate. The shaman was the guardian of the psychic life of the community, combating demons of the inner life as well as disease. As a mediator between the comprehensible and the non-comprehensible, the unnameable, the shaman could make a perilous world seem manageable.

Shamanism around the world

SIBERIA

Siberia includes many tribes such as the most numerous Buryat and Yakut, with the Goldi, Chukchee, Kirghiz, Uighur, Altaian, Evenk and others. It has been said that the reason so many tribal customs have survived in this area is because of its sheer inhospitability to invaders! Although the word 'shaman' is probably derived from the Tungusic, as we have seen, much of the current recovery of shamanic ways derives from the native North Americans. There has been – and still is – considerable argument over what actually defines 'shamanism', for the term has been applied quite loosely to all types of trance states and folk-magic, and Siberian customs do not always have considerable relevance to what we seek today.

Siberian shamans were chosen by the spirits, although it helped if someone in the family had also been a shaman. After a period of crisis the shaman emerged stronger, although Dr. Hutton (see 'Further Reading') tells us 'The degree of recovery was not always complete, for some Siberian shamans were quite clearly demented...' Nonetheless, the shaman still knew well what to do. After election there followed a period of training by an existing shaman. Subsequently came acceptance by the tribe, which was not always guaranteed, followed by a ceremony of consecration. Costume and equipment were of great importance, and shamanic 'seances' were energetic and dramatic events. Shamans dealt with mysterious diseases or inexplicable bad luck. It was a vocation that was not sought, for it was a lonely, uncertain occupation conveying disgrace if success was elusive and other, more subtle dangers such as destruction, in the spirit world, by a rival shaman. When we look closely at Siberian shamanism we may find little to inspire our modern quest. Nonetheless, native customs are generally sources of wisdom and alternative perspectives.

australia

The Australian Aboriginal culture is very ancient, extending back at least 40,000 years. The spirits of the Dreamtime choose the candidate shaman, piercing his head from ear to ear and spiking his tongue and neck with invisible lances. One of the most interesting aspects of Aboriginal shamanism is the belief in the power of crystals. These may be 'inserted' on a journey into the body of the novice, so conferring special abilities. (Needless to say, these techniques have symbolic meaning – you should not think of attempting them yourself.) Crystals are regarded as pieces of solidified light, celestial in origin, and so their presence enables the initiate to ascend to the sky. Baiame, the All-Father, sits on a throne of transparent crystal, and he bestows shamanic powers on dreamers by drenching them in a waterfall of liquid quartz. They grow wings and are able to fly. Baiame then inserts a piece of quartz into their forehead, endowing them with X-ray vision. Different tribes have specific myths and traditions, but are strongly shamanic in nature, by most definitions, incorporating spirit-flight and mastery over fire.

the orient

Here shamanism predates the advent of Buddhism and Confucianism, and shamans were persecuted by these newer religions in China in the first century. The drum is used in Tibet to this day for purposes of spirit-flight and soul-retrieval, and it is believed that in times past a sacred rope linked Earth and the sky-dwelling of the gods. The meditative practices of Taoism have something in common with shamanism, as does the experience of mystical unity and spirit journeys, undertaken by Taoists. Shamanism is still practised in remote regions of Japan, and this may have originated from the influence of Siberian tribes.

south america and mexico

The shamanic tradition of these countries is characterised by the use of hallucinogens. South America in particular is home to the

'curanderos' – healers – whose habits are close to shamanism. There are many stories of notable cures, and the Peruvian curandero, Eduardo Calderon, is one of the best-known figures. Calderon uses the psychedelic effects of the San Pedro cactus to arrive at diagnoses, and then to exorcise the cause. His rites involve both Christian and native elements. It is not unusual to find a mixture of mythologies in these countries. For instance, the chant of Maria Sabina, quoted in part at the chapter heading, also calls on Jesus and Mary. The Indians of Meso-America believe that Christ once walked upon their mountains, and from his blood grew the holy mushrooms that are ingested to promote trance. This is a variation on the legend of Quetzalcoatl, the feathered serpent god of Central America, who was the giver of breath and god of the winds. He was both a solar, creator god, and a god who descended to the land of the dead. Recovering, he gathered up his bones, returned to the Earth and sprinkled them with his own blood, so turning them into human beings. Both Jesus Christ and Quetzalcoatl represent regeneration, and the ecstatic perceives the essential oneness behind all myths.

NORTh AMERICA

There is a lively tradition of shamanism among the Eskimo, who regard the principal tasks of the shaman to be that of healing and also undertaking undersea journeys to the Mother of the Sea Beasts to ensure a plentiful supply of game. The ecstatic journey to the sky, or the bottom of the sea, may reveal where taboos have been breached that have brought ill fortune to the people. Eskimo shamans have their bodies bound by a rope while in the trance state, so they are not carried bodily into the sky, never to be seen again.

However, it is from the native North American Indians that the modern shamanic revival draws its principal inspiration. Mircea Eliade (see 'Further Reading') has this to say:

We have shown that every Indian seeks religious power, that every Indian commands a guardian spirit acquired by the same techniques that the shaman uses to obtain his own spirits. The difference between layman and shaman is quantitative; the shaman commands a greater number of tutelary or guardian spirits and a

*stronger magico-religious 'power'. In this respect we could say
that every Indian 'shamanizes' even if he does not consciously
wish to become a shaman.*

Native American shamans are concerned with healing and soul-
flight in ways similar to those we have already encountered. Among
the North Americans however, vision quest is more common, and a
visionary quality infuses the culture in a way that has provoked the
envy of Westerners, who have well-nigh destroyed this proud and
enlightened race. The native Americans have much to offer the
impoverished souls of the developed world. Some natives feel
justifiably resentful at the way their traditions have been ransacked,
but others are happy that their wisdom is able to infiltrate other
races and that the spirit of the Redman may endure in another guise
– which is what some legends lead us to believe was the intention.
Whatever may be the case, we can only ever borrow from this rich
treasure house, and hopefully we can repay in some fashion that
may benefit the Earth. American traditions appear in several places
in the pages of this book.

PRACTICE

If you are interested in learning more about shamanism in
anthropological and historical contexts, you may like to begin with
some of the books listed in 'Further Reading'. These works contain
their own bibliographies and lists of resources that can take your
exploration further, if you so wish.

3

THE MEDICINE
WHEEL

*... Good Lance ... placed one rock first in the centre of the pit,
then four rocks around it, then one more rock on top of the
middle one. These represented the earth, the four directions of the
universe, and the sky ...*

Leonard Crow Dog, Sioux medicine man

The medicine wheel is a symbol of wholeness, of perfection, balance
and completeness. Nature doesn't create straight lines – it moves in
circles. The Earth is circular, it turns round on its axis, it goes round
the sun, the sun and moon appear circular in the sky. The cycle of
the seasons is like an ever-repeating circle, going round and round.
The passage from birth to death to rebirth is circular – or perhaps we
should say it is a spiral and that the circle is a cross-section of a spiral,
enabling us to see the stages of one loop. It is even said that space

is circular, so that the traveller, after aeons of light years moving in a straight line from where he started would find himself at length back where he began.

So the wheel has many significances. The medicine wheel is also a philosophical system, a map or compass to help us find our way, to orienteer and ground us when we embark on inner journeys, and it gives protection through its metaphorical power. Medicine in this sense means power. The medicine wheel is a power wheel, showing separate forces in complete balance. The medicine wheel exists inside us and outside us – it makes up our being, and it makes up the cosmos. We can use it to understand ourselves, and to understand life, to fix our place in the world, and the spirit, and to form a framework to honour the natural forces and tides of being.

In this way the wheel is an altar, a centering device for our consciousness, a sacred space, an aid to meditation. The wheel has many meanings, on many different levels, and all that exists has a place on the wheel. Jamie Sams and David Carson have this to say: 'All space is sacred space. Every inch of Mother Earth holds a specially energized connection to some living creature, and is therefore to be honoured. The Medicine Wheel is a physical expression of this knowledge, and can be used to set up sacred ceremonial space.' (*Medicine Cards* – see 'Further Reading'.) The medicine wheel is indeed a place of beauty and balance, and in setting it up we make many statements and open many doors.

The medicine wheel is similar to the circle of power used by Western occultists. Here the emphasis is sometimes on directing forces rather than identifying with them, but in essence there is little difference, for no true 'directing' can be achieved without a deep understanding so that we hardly direct at all– for an important part of the process is that we identify purpose, of which we may then become a part. In exploring the wheel we can hope to understand ourselves and the world better, more vividly, metaphorically, poetically and pictorially. The medicine wheel is another way of bringing existence to life and discerning meaning. It defines where we are in space and time and where we are going/have been. Also by its very essence it conveys that past, future, earth and sky, here and there are all part of a cosmic pattern, and essentially form a unity.

Here I would like to look at two wheels – the traditional Western model and that taken from the Lakota native American tradition. There are also other wheels. I give two wheels for the sake of information and so that you can make a choice based on your own feelings. You may like to research further before you make up your mind, and for this you may like to start with some of the books in 'Further Reading'. Part of the exercises given at the end of the chapter concern forming your own impressions and composing your own 'wheel'. However, there are two points to be borne in mind.

First, if you wish to embark on solo work it is entirely up to you which wheel you choose. However, if you become part of a group you will need to be able to identify with the wheel used by your group. It may be hard to change mid-stream if you have begun a little work on your own and then join others who are operating differently, for calling up the four quarters of the wheel is usually an important step in workings, and sets the atmosphere powerfully and evocatively.

Second, I urge you very strongly to work with one version of the wheel for a year at least, and unless you are working very intensively several years would be recommended. There comes a time when the meanings of the wheel are deeply embedded in you and your life. At this point you may choose to explore other versions, and this may expand your awareness and be very stimulating – but only if the first wheel is so much a part of you that it is second nature. If you wish to go well below the surface of things – and this is sure to be the case if you embark on shamanic work – then you will understand that some things take time and deserve respect. Respect the wheel for its beauty and power and give it time to become part of you.

The Lakota wheel

The version of the wheel frequently used comes from the Lakota tradition, but there are many variations upon this, and none is 'right' or 'wrong', although one may be right for a particular person at a particular time. The basic version of the wheel divides it into

four quarters which correspond to the four cardinal directions. The quartered circle, which is the same as the Celtic cross, is an ancient sign of wholeness – or 'holiness'.

EAST

The Eastern quarter is the direction of sunrise, and we may visualise ourselves 'entering' the wheel as we entered upon our physical incarnation, from this point. The element of the East is Fire, and the colour yellow. The totem beast of the East is the soaring, far-sighted Eagle, and the heavenly body associated with it is the Sun.

The wheel not only represents orienteering in terms of direction. It also represents the passage of day into night and back to the dawn again. Likewise it plots the rhythm of the year, through spring, summer, autumn, winter and back again to the freshness of spring. Human life, too, is depicted, from birth, through youth, maturity, death and rebirth, for it is evident to the awakened vision that life does not begin at birth and end at death – all is circular, repeating, metamorphosing, and repeating once more on a higher octave of the spiral.

East is the first clarion call of dawn, it is spring, and it brings the quality of enlightenment. This is the moment of incarnation, of entry into matter. East is equated with the Kingdom of Humanity (as opposed to plants, animals and minerals) and specifically, for humans, it is related to that quality in us that we may call spirit, or perhaps intuition, in the sense that the psychologist C.G. Jung used the term. This is the ability to perceive overall meanings and purposes, to go with inspiration and to 'see' around corners, for to the holistic vision corners sometimes don't exist. The enemy of the East is death and old age, not in their sense of wisdom and transformation, but in their restrictive meanings of loss of sight, movement and potential, and their bequest of fear. In the East we determine how we will use energies on all levels. It is the 'far-sighted place' and is perhaps the most abstract of the quarters.

South

After the East we come, clockwise, to the South. In the Northern Hemisphere we usually move clockwise in a ritual context, for that is the direction of the sun's movement. The reverse is true in the Southern Hemisphere, of course. Equally the meanings of South and North may be reversed as the medicine wheel is rotated through 180° to be more suitable to the Southern Hemisphere.

South is linked to midday, to summer and to the colour red. This is the time of youth, a time when we trust, when we are innocent, and when we are preoccupied with how we feel and what is close to us, so in human terms South corresponds to the emotions. The element of the South is Water and the heavenly body is the Moon, ruler of the tides. The totem beast of the South is the Mouse, which may

seem a humble animal. However, all creatures are of equal value in truth and all have a message for us and qualities we may learn from. With Mouse we learn the importance of close observation, of really *being* who and where we are, which is necessary for us to make intelligent choices. We may equate the South with the Jungian function of Feeling, that identifies what is of worth and meaning to us, to our loved ones, and the society we live in. Feeling brings comfort, unifies and encourages cultural growth. The enemy of the South is fear, that kills our ability to make decisions and keeps us in one place, quivering. South represents the plant kingdom, the givers of energy, and it is the 'close to' place.

WEST

We come now to the West, direction of the element Earth, evening and autumn. The colour of the West is black, and it is the home of the mineral kingdom – the infinitely slow, silent life that is closest to earth. The human aspect concerns the physical body and so we may link it with Jung's Sensation function – the use of the five ordinary senses, the 'real'. And so the West corresponds to maturity – a time when we have the strength to do things, to help others both young and old in practical, active ways. However, the West is also about deep introspection, about intuition, too, but of a more inward sort than the East, and transition from one state to another. Its totem beast is the Grizzly Bear, strongest of the bears, self-healing through its instinctive knowledge of herbs and aware of the need to prepare for the future as it eats and stocks up for hibernation in winter. The heavenly body associated with West is the Earth, and its enemy is powerlessness. The West is the realm of the holders of energy, the 'looks within' place.

NORTH

Finally we come to the North, where the colour is white, as of the snow and the season is winter. North corresponds to midnight, and the heavenly body is the Stars. The element of the North is Air, and we can associate that with knowledge and wisdom – the Jungian Thinking function which clarifies and classifies so leading at its best to profound understanding. In human terms this is the realm of the mind (which is not the same as the brain), and it is associated with

receivers of energy, the animal kingdom. The totem beast for the North is the Buffalo, whose northern European equivalent would have been the wild ox. The buffalo was of vital importance to the native Americans, for all parts of it were used – its meat for food, its hide for clothes and tipis, its bones for weapons and utensils. Buffalo were not exploited, they were honoured, as all animals, as manifestations of the Great Spirit. Herds of buffalo moving across the plains reflect the mobility of air and the many uses of the buffalo depict the adaptability of the element. Corresponding to old age and death, and also to the indefinable time between incarnations, the North is the 'place of knowledge'. Significantly, its enemy is certainty.

Setting out the wheel

The wheel may be – and indeed should be – set out physically as an aid to meditation or a prelude to journeying. This can be done using a circular mat, a coffee table, tray or whatever comes to hand. A compass is not necessary in your own home, for the directions need only be more or less correct. However, if it is night-time in an unfamiliar location, you may wish to take a compass to be sure.

It is important to go with your feelings in representing the wheel. What do you associate with South? with North? and so on. Some suggestions for what you might wish to place at the four points on your circular locus might be:

East A bundle of candles tied in a yellow ribbon; an egg (either ornamental or real); pictures of sunrise; anything yellow or bright; anything specifically human and speaking of enlightenment, for instance Leonard da Vinci's *Universal Man* or Blake's *The Ancient of Days*, bird feathers.

South Water in a red bowl; anything red; a plant; an ornament showing the Moon; pictures of plants; even a piece of cheese! (to link with mice and milk).

West Here you could put all manner of stones, precious and otherwise; nuts and herbs; a bowl containing soil; artefacts in black; a print of a bear's paw.

North   Anything white, suggesting snow, mountaintops, clarity; figures of animals, especially buffalo; butterflies; sycamore keys (and any other wind-born seeds); representations of a council of elders; star-charts. Here joss-sticks may be burnt, or placed as a representation of incense, the gift of Air.

In the **centre** you may like to light a candle, in acknowledgement of the presence of Spirit. After you light your candle, remember only to move sunwise in the presence of your medicine wheel as a mark of respect for the forces you are honouring.

Above, below and centre

Our wheel has been two dimensional, but we do well to remember the three other positions that form our place in the universe and are also relevant to our journeying, in Middleworld, Upperworld and Lowerworld.

Above is the realm of Father Sky, who shows us ways we can expand, become greater, find relevance, meaning and enlightenment. Father Sky calls us to move, spiritually, conceptually, and materially. Like a good Earthly father his love is always present, but his approval is conditional. He does not set standards for us, but he encourages us to find our own yardstick and to develop, making the best of ourselves in our own way.

Below is the realm of the Earth Mother, home of our ancestry and our instinctual power. Earth Mother shows us ways to our depths, to our deepest sources and helps us to access all the hidden talents that are our birthright. Like a good Earthly mother her love is always available, and her acceptance is unconditional, but she asks that we truly accept ourselves, and face ourselves with honesty and courage so that we may grow.

The centre is the place of stillness, poise and quietude. It is the ever-pregnant void, the emptiness within us where we may hear the 'still, small voice'. It has also been linked to the fifth, most subtle

element, ether, that informs and interpenetrates the other four elements. The centre is the totality of the year, the cycle, the cosmos. It is the place of spirituality and imagination, and we may link it to our sexuality as a function within us that generates new life, inspiration, poetry, and sends us on a quest for wholeness.

Calling up the directions

Find your own ways of calling upon the directions, when you set up your wheel. Close your eyes and utter what comes into your head – any pictures, associations, feelings or even poetry. For instance, for the South you might say:

> 'Spirit of the South, I ask you to be present with me today. Warmth, lush greenery, beauty – I travel in your embrace. Help me to find the child within me and to notice all the small, humble things that are so important. May the Moon sway the tides of my soul and may I walk fearlessly, and with trust.'

For the rest I am sure you can make up your own words, on the basis of your own reactions. Don't forget to call upon Father Sky, Mother Earth and the centre, also. Then allow the peace and sense of completeness generated to permeate you, in preparation for the tasks ahead.

The four directions are perhaps better understood as intelligent cosmic forces of great magnitude. They are not confined to the designated quarters – rather these directions are used as a means of approaching and contacting them.

The wheel can also be used therapeutically. For instance, you may feel you need to cheer up, to learn to be more playful, more interested in your surroundings and to receive the innocence and spontaneity you knew as a child, So, with this in mind, having laid out your wheel and called upon the directions, you may decide to 'sit in the South' in order to absorb the qualities of the South, to become warmer, more youthful, more simple.

The Western wheel

Briefly, now, let us look at the version of the wheel that is used by Western occultists and those involved in ritual, esoteric work. This wheel is more fully explained in *Witchcraft – a beginner's guide* in this series. It is more usual to 'conjure' the four quarters of the wheel and to imagine oneself inside a protective circle with the four Guardians (i.e the elemental powers) at the four cardinal points. Representations of the elements may be placed on an altar, which is generally placed in the North in the Northern Hemisphere, and candles may be put on the perimeter. When the circle has been created and the elements invoked the scene is set for whatever rite is to follow, Present-day shamanic groups do not use the wheel in the same way, but when examined the principles are essentially the same. These are the elemental associations, which as you will see are connected with symbols/vessels rather than animals.

North

This is the 'blind side' of the sky in the Northern Hemisphere, where the sun and moon are never seen and where the circumpolar stars delineate the Silver Wheel of the goddess Arianrhod, where souls retreat between incarnations. North is the abode of Earth, of magic and realised intention. In general it corresponds to the same as West on the Lakota wheel, although it is associated with midnight, old age/death/reincarnation and midwinter. North is usually invoked first. Its symbols are stone, and pentacle, which is a disk engraved usually with a five-point star.

East

Home of sunrise, clarity and light, East is associated with Air, the powers of thought, youth, spring, morning. Its symbols are the censer, which dispenses incense, and the sword or ritual knife, which represent the cutting, differentiating power of the mind. Generally it resembles North on the Lakota wheel, although day,

year and lifetime associations are different. East is usually invoked second, as we move in a clockwise direction.

South

If we live in the north, South is the abode of heat, passion, life – it is the direction of fiery arrows of intuition, the flames of inspiration. Generally it is similar to East on the Lakota wheel, although it is linked to young adulthood, summer and midday. Its symbols are the candle and the wand, although certain traditions reverse the symbols for East and South. South is usually invoked third, although in the Southern Hemisphere associations may be rotated through 180° and South invoked first.

West

Realm of the sunset, the blessed Isles of the Dead, direction of the underworld of the heart and the cosmos, West is associated with Water and emotion. Its symbols are the chalice and the cauldron. It has little of the flavour of the Lakota South, for here there is maturity, reflection, melancholy, empathy and profound joy also. The West corresponds to evening, autumn and maturity.

It can be seen that the Western wheel rotates the Lakota wheel one notch, and yet the associations cannot be simply moved along. Notably, there is little to correspond to the 'close to' place, in the South of the Lakota. The account given here is brief. It is only when this wheel/circle is used for ritual, especially based on the turning of the seasons, that it comes to life in all its beauty. For instance, at Hallowe'en (also called Samhain) ritual tends to centre on the West, the home of the Ancestors and the spirits of the departed. The Underworld God is visualised as coming from this direction, and the Wise Crone aspect of the Goddess. Thus the West holds all the witchery of the dying evening light, the twisted thorn tree denuded by winter gales, the enchanted depths of a forest pool.

Give yourself time to decide which version of the wheel appeals to you. The Practice at the end may help you to make contact with your own associations.

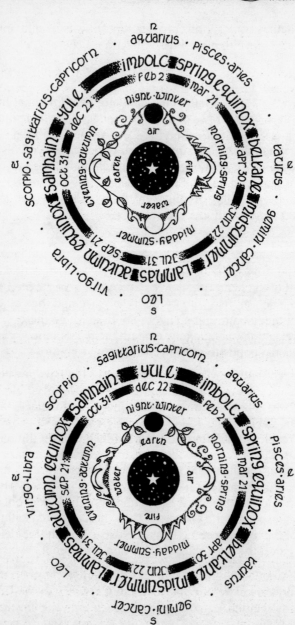

The Wheel of the Year

We have seen how the seasons correlate with the medicine wheel. In addition, we can have a wheel with eight segments, incorporating the Equinoxes, Solstices, and the points between them marked by the ancient Celtic festivals of Beltane (30 April), Lammas (31 July), Samhain (31 October) and Imbolc (2 February). Yule (Midwinter Solstice) or Imbolc are then placed at the northernmost point, and the others placed round in sequence. We can then bear in mind the associations and mythology of the festivals and seasons in connection with the meanings of the wheel. The Wheel of the Year is fully explored in *The Wheel of the Year – Myth and Magic Through the Seasons*, also published by Hodder & Stoughton.

The phases of the moon

These too can be plotted in relation to the medicine wheel, with the dark of the moon corresponding to North, waxing to East, full to South and waning to West. The rhythms of the moon are vital, if often overlooked in our lives, and the theme of transformation and rebirth of dark moon connected to North, burgeoning and growing of waxing moon to East, fulfilment and culmination of full moon to South and introspection and retraction of waning moon to West can be added to our understanding of the quarters.

The twelve astrological signs

These too can be placed on the wheel, dividing it into twelve sections. If we place Imbolc in the North, then our northernmost point falls in the centre of Aquarius, with Capricorn to the left/west and Pisces to the right/east. These three then form the Northern triad, with Aries, Taurus and Gemini the Eastern triad, Cancer, Leo

and Virgo the Southern triad and finally Libra, Scorpio and Sagittarius the Western triad. Or we may prefer to place Capricorn as beginning at the midwinter solstice at the top right-hand portion (NNE) and so continue round. This is a fertile idea, as each of the zodiacal signs is associated with its own element. Thus we have Capricorn (Earth) on the Air portion of the Lakota wheel, giving another dimension to the Capricorn character. The Fire sign, Leo, then falls in the most southerly position, in the Water element on the Lakota wheel, enabling us to think in new ways about Leo, and so on with each of the zodiacal signs.

Let us begin in a simple way, in our Practice section.

PRACTICE

In more 'authentic' tribal settings the lore of the wheel would not be taught in this way. Rather it would be conveyed wordlessly – a matter of instinct, absorption, exploration and a knowledge that welled up from within, in addition to coming from without. We do not have the opportunity to develop in this way, in our culture, but we can still work towards an understanding of the wheel that goes far beyond the intellect.

Our practice involves setting up your own wheel. Take your time with this. Particularly if you are intending to work alone, take the time to develop your own associations, which may be different from either of the above. Spend time outside, in areas close to where you live. Which is the most prevailing wind direction at each time of the year? From where does the cold, wintery air come, from where the hot breath of summer? What do you associate with these times, these directions? If you do not feel sure of your feelings set out to walk in the direction of your choice and see what you encounter. Do you see many birds flying, hear them singing, find their nests? Or do you encounter scuttling, creeping creatures, tall trees, much undergrowth? What about cloud pictures, rainbows, threads of smoke from bonfires? And people you meet – what are they like? How do you feel?

Note all of these things and see if they inspire you to certain associations.

When you feel happy about your conclusions then draw your own wheel, complete with colours and associations. Make a large wheel on a piece of A4 paper, divide it into sections and make drawings, jottings, whatever appeals. Make notes for each of your sections, listing all that you feel relevant. You may want to do this several times, make several wheels.

Having completed this section of the work, now it is time to build your stone circle. This can be as large or as small as you wish. If you have a big garden you may like to construct a circle with large stones outside. Or you may wish to use tiny stones, on a tray or tablemat. When you go out looking for your stones, look in a northerly direction, for instance, for your North stone, and find one that is white in colour. Similarly with the other directions. You can buy semi-precious stones if you wish. Do anything that appeals. You can embellish your circle with stones between each of the four, to make eight in number, and have a central stone also. Do not forget to orientate your stones fairly accurately to the directions if you are placing them outside. Stand at the East stone for sunrise, at the West for sunset. Absorb the glory of noon with your South stone and face North at midnight, with the moon behind you, casting your shadow over your Northern stone. Use your stones to help you attune more fully with the world around you, as part of your shamanic development. When you are ready to journey, your medicine wheel background will be an important source of orienteering and making connection, in the Otherworld.

Finally, let the medicine wheel become part of your life in day-to-day living. My friend Jan, one of our group leaders, who is devoted to and experienced in shamanic work, has a version of the medicine wheel in magnets on her fridge! This wheel isn't just for ritual purposes. The way of the shaman sees ritual as life, life as ritual, all is connected in metaphor and practice, and spirituality is not confined to prescribed days and places – it is for always and ever-present, to enrich us and enlarge us and fill us with joy.

So the medicine wheel is a concept that we can get started with, but almost has no limits as to how we may play with it in order to make the most useful, inspiring associations. Brooke Medicine Eagle, a North American medicine woman, has these words:

> *We need to achieve a clarity and a lack of resistance before we seek vision – a surrendering, a relinquishing. If you are unwilling to be in your experience now, then vision will not open for you. You need to get on that circle where there is no resistance, no up, no down, where there are no square corners to stumble on. Then, someday, you become that circle …*

4

shamanic cosmology

To see a World in a grain of sand,
And a Heaven in a wild flower,
Hold Infinity in the palm of your hand,
And Eternity in an hour

William Blake

The map and the country

When we make a journey into unfamiliar territory we need a map – a chart to enable us to get our bearings, to make sense of our position and to help us decide which route to take. The medicine wheel that we encountered in the previous chapter is an important map, but it is two dimensional. Shamanic journeys are multidimensional, and no map can encompass this. However, we can find a helpful framework to take us upwards and downwards, and to help to orientate us when we leave the world of the everyday.

It must be remembered at all times, however, that 'the map is not the country'. This is a phrase coined by the psychologist C.G. Jung, in respect of his own theories about the human psyche. No map is infallible, or even 'right' in an eternal, doctrinal fashion. Maps are intended to help, not to confine. They are only part of the story and they may fail to take into account certain significant points on the journey. For instance, a road map will not tell you about roadworks you may encounter. It may not show one-way streets. There may have been new roads built since it was published, or old ones may have fallen into disrepair. A map will not indicate whether the road surface is smooth or bumpy, whether there is a speed limit or special hazards – so a map has limits. In addition, maps of the same terrain can look very different, according to what is featured. An ordnance survey map will show aspects of the landscape that would not be found on a road map, and vice versa.

Alternative cosmologies

Maps of the Otherworld are similar in that they can help you, but they cannot describe what you may encounter, or prepare you fully for it. Different traditions have different maps, and the experiences of the shaman often support the beliefs of her culture – because that is the map she has journeyed by. This does not mean that one map is right and the other wrong, or that the shamanic experience is suspect or invalid. It just means that we use certain ways to make

sense of things to our conscious minds, and these ways may differ. We can consider reports of 'Near Death Experience' in the same way. The visions encountered tend to coincide with the beliefs of the culture. For instance, a Christian might meet an angel, whereas a tribesman might encounter his totem beast. Beyond the superficial there is little difference – both are powerful, both exist in an alternative dimension and both are helpful. Indeed, they may be one and the same being, seen in a different guise. Kenneth Meadows (*Where Eagles Fly* – see 'Further Reading') encapsulates it thus: 'Truth wears many masks in order to teach us not to mistake appearances for the reality'.

The map of the Otherworld that we shall consider here is a general one, based on no special culture or belief, but encompassing three worlds – the Upper, Middle and Lower. The concept of three worlds is one that appears in most cosmologies, and usually, but not always, humans inhabit the Middleworld. The three levels may be linked by a sacred river or road, or a great tree. Perhaps the best-known tree in this respect is Yggdrasil, the World Tree of Norse myth. This huge tree grows from the lower world, Hel, through Midgard and its branches rise into the upper realms of the gods, Asgard.

In contrast, the Siberian Evenks – a culture with a strong shamanic tradition – see the levels linked by the Clan River. This river rises in the Upperworld, where the creator god, Amaka, resides with Eksheri, master of beasts, birds and fish and god of the hunt. In the lower world the souls of the dead live, along with spirits of disease, and the Clan Mistress, who also rules the hunt. This Clan Mistress, half human and half animal, suggests much about our sources of strength and inspiration, which we shall be considering when we examine the Lowerworld.

Middleworld

This is the world we inhabit in an everyday sense – but not quite! We are closest to true Middleworld at dusk, or dawn, when we are drifting and daydreaming, when we catch sight of things from the

corner of the eye that aren't 'really' there, when we sense atmospheres, see ghosts, or generally when we feel close to nature. Middleworld is there when we see the bobbing tale of a rabbit, and realise that the field is alive with these vibrant, shy creatures that disappear into the soil itself when disturbed. Middleworld is glimpsed in the flash of a fox's tail, whisking behind a hedge. Middleworld is the scrape and squelch of the questing root as it spirals into the earth – a sound that is beyond the limits of our normal hearing. And Middleworld is the whisper of the wind and the song of the stream. It is the world within the world, behind the world, that we can so easily miss, with our tunnel vision.

Cultivating a true sense of Middleworld involves recognition that nature is not our slave, but our mother, and that in many respects rampant technology has cut us off from our lifeblood. When we imagine a Golden Age, that is Middleworld – this world as it is, should or could be, as it was before humans lost contact with their soul, before they interfered so grossly in all that should have inspired an overwhelming respect. The true beauty of the Earth is still there, in Middleworld, and we can visit it in shamanic journeying. So Middleworld is both our 'ordinary' world and the world as seen through the eyes of the mystic.

We can equate Middleword both with our day-to-day consciousness and with what we could call the subconscious – that part of ourselves that isn't perpetually 'with' us but which we can recall fairly easily – memories, dreams, feelings. When people undertake guided visualisations they are often travelling in Middleworld, exploring the dimensions of their experience and imagination without going too deep. Middleworld journeys can involve going back – or possibly forwards – in time and they relate to current issues. A client telling a therapist about his relationship with his father is in a sense making a Middleworld journey, although this is distinct from the shamanic journey in that it is not nearly so vivid, present, and all-enveloping. Patients in a hypnotic trance who are asked by the therapist to imagine themselves by a cool stream, on a high hill or by a lake are taking a type of Middleworld journey. If we visit sacred sites, wells and standing stones to experience their true powers and meanings, again we are making a type of Middleworld journey that will help when we embark on true shamanic journeying. Shamanic journeys begin in a special Middleworld location, as we shall be examining later.

(MIDDLEWORLD CREATURES

The creatures encountered in the Middleworld may be totem or guardian animals, nature spirits and such goddesses and gods that are especially associated with the powers of the earth – for example, the Earth Mother and her mythic champions like King Arthur. Herne the Hunter, the Green Man, Pan, Demeter – all these are 'earthy'

deities, although one must remember that god-forms have a multidimensional existence.

The nature spirits or elementals fall into four types. Earth spirits are called gnomes, Air spirits sylphs, Water spirits undines and Fire spirits salamanders. You can sense or even see these creatures at certain times and certain locations, and they all have their own powers or gifts that we can ask to partake of, to help us. If we ask sincerely, with respect, and we are ready also to give back, we are usually rewarded.

MIDDLEWORLD PRACTICE

We have already discussed the importance of a certain amount of practicality and 'groundedness' as we develop our shamanic skills. We can emphasise this when we affirm our connection with Middleworld. Generally this involves fulfilling our commitments, maintaining a reasonable level of attention to what we have decided is suitable for us, and caring for our bodies and those of our nearest and dearest, where appropriate. Here are some further suggestions.

1 Select one healing task per day (or week, if you are very busy), so much the better if this involves the earth, plants or animals. This could involve anything from simply watering the garden, to visiting a sick friend in hospital. It may mean taking yourself to a quiet location in order to benefit from the healing energies there. It may mean taking the dog for a walk, planting seeds, choosing a present. Whatever it is, do it with the intention of making yourself, a friend, a pet or the earth more 'whole'. Make a routine of this.

2 Practise with the medicine wheel that we explored in the previous chapter, in any way you like – draw it, sing it, dance it – be as creative as you like.

3 Contact with the elementals: if you are fortunate enough to have an open fire you can sit and look within the embers for 'fire-pictures' – or you can build a bonfire or just light a candle. Feel the transformative, sizzling energies of the salamanders – call on them if your courage and inspiration are flagging.

The undines can be found by lakeside, in streams and pools. Look into the green and blue depths. Simply place water in a bowl if you can't go out. Call on the undines for renewal, for healing, for that soothing feeling that pervades when you are in harmony with yourself, with the depths of your own soul, and when you feel loved.

Gnomes can be found in caves, but they are also there when you do the garden and go for walks. Feel the firm earth under your feet, smell the soil, hold a stone in your palm and call on the gnomes for their protection and common sense and to help you with practical and arduous tasks.

Sylphs travel in the breeze and fly among tree-branches and high places. Find them on windswept hills, see them in the clouds. Simply open your window and invite them in on the stream of fresh air. Sylphs can give you a clear mind and help your powers of logic and communication – call on them for these, when you need them.

Finally, give back when and where you can. Pouring wine or water on the earth is a remembrance of her bounty, lighting a joss-stick is a celebration of the gifts of air and fire, planting seeds is a big 'thank you'. If you can do nothing else at present, just sing a song of joy into the wind, and let it be carried away by the sylphs, where they wish.

4 Travelling a cycle: Choose either a day or a lunar month, depending how much time you have to spare and how much work you feel you need to do on your awareness of natural rhythms. Chart the fluctuations of energy, the movements, the differences that appear during your timescale. If you have chosen a day you will need to devote much of the day to this. For instance, when it is morning ask yourself how it feels, what is the day like, the air, the sun's position, heat, light and so on. What is your mood? Make a note of all these things – daydream, dance, play music, eat, drink – talk into a tape recorder saying all the thoughts that arise about this particular here-and-now. Be as aware as you can all day, but continue also with routine tasks, for they are the bedrock of life. Take a note of how things

change as noon approaches, afternoon, dusk, nightfall. And now the moon rises … Note how different things look by moonlight, how differently you respond to it.

If you have chosen a lunar month, start at new moon and note your dreams, fluctuations in energy and activity, your moods and those of friends and family, plant growth, news items, weather and anything that you particularly notice. If you are a woman note also your menstrual cycle. It is a good idea to do both of these cycles – day and month – and see how they compare. They will help to ensure your contact with the energies that empower Middleworld.

Lowerworld

I have purposely referred to the 'Lowerworld', rather than the Underworld. That is because there are many negative associations attached to this area, and any term that takes us further away from associations with hell is to be recommended. The cosmos of the shaman contains no such place, nor does it contain an evil force, such as the devil. However, this does not mean that malevolence doesn't exist or that everything and everyone that we may meet on our shamanic journeys is helpful, or well disposed towards us.

When we begin considering Lowerworld we have to shed the ideas of our culture that associate this with fear, damnation and evil and have made it a kind of cosmic 'dustbin'. Lowerworld is, in fact, a place of great power, where we can draw on ancestral gifts, find our transformative powers, our 'gut feelings' and our links with our roots. Caitlin Matthews (*Singing the Soul Back Home* – see 'Further Reading') has this to say: 'The Underworld is the power-house of the three worlds. Here we draw upon our deep resources, our traditional inheritance, our memory … When we enter the Underworld, we too put down our tap-root and draw up refreshment'.

In terms of ideas of the World Tree, Lowerworld is, of course, the place of roots. We can also link it to the reptilian brain stem and all

the gifts and mysteries of our lineage, back through apes, reptiles, plants and back to the dawn of time, when we were molecules floating in the endless void, looking for the embrace of a soil that would nurture us, and enable us to grow. All true growth begins in the secrecy of Lowerworld, and we may link this world with our unconscious minds, those recesses deep within us that we find hard to locate but which in many ways control our lives. Creativity begins in Lowerworld.

Deities of Lowerworld include Celtic figures like the goddess Cerridwen, with her Cauldron of Transformation, the Horned God Cernunnos (who is an aspect of Herne the Hunter), Ereshkigal, Hecate and Persephone/Kore and her consort Pluto. Most cultures have myths of heroes and heroines who make an underworld journey in search of strength, knowledge and rebirth. Orpheus in search of Eurydice, and the goddess Inanna confronting her underworld sister, Ereshkigal, are two such. Spirits of the ancestors also inhabit Lowerworld, with totem animals and strange and monstrous beasts and guardians.

Lowerworld is also the home of all that is feared and repressed, whether culturally or personally – or both. To quote Caitlin Matthews once more '... here the threshold guardians assume tiny or gigantic size, here we meet the spirits of realities we have neglected or ignored ...'. These have to be reclaimed, at some stage, if we are to progress, in an initiatory experience that may be very frightening.

There is a saying worth remembering in connection with this: 'Where there's fear, there's power'. This means several things: It means that when we fear something we give it power over us – a power it could never otherwise possess. It also means that we are giving away something of ourselves in the process, for much energy is sucked into the fear-vortex, leaving us depleted and confused. Most importantly, the degree to which we fear a thing is an indication of the power that is really ours, that we can and must reclaim. Strangely, things we fear usually represent elements within ourselves that we have repressed. Mostly these traits and abilities are essentially positive but for some reason, probably linked to

conditioning, we cannot handle them. So we turn them into monsters instead. An enormous amount of personal power can remain dammed up and distorted in this way, and it is in Lowerworld that we may find a way of releasing it.

Lowerworld journeys can be difficult, and so it may be best not to attempt them until you have acquired some experience and spirit allies to accompany you, and have a support framework of people with whom you can discuss your experiences. Especially if you have a background of belief in devils, hell and eternal punishment, Lowerworld may present problems – and these associations are as hard to eradicate as dandelion roots, for when you think they are thoroughly gone, up they pop in another place and they have to be sorted all over again. Bear this in mind and be gentle with yourself. Keep affirming to yourself that it is okay to leave these negative associations behind you.

Ultimately, Lowerworld journeys can help us come to terms with death and with our own death, and this is one of the long-term goals of true shamanic work.

Lowerworld journeys

Lowerworld is usually approached via a 'tunnel', and we shall be discussing how you can enter this in our 'General Practice' at the end of the chapter. However, when you enter Lowerworld, you will find that in many respects it looks the same as Middleworld, although the beings encountered there are likely to be different.

Some of the most memorable journeys I have undertaken concerned meeting animals in Lowerworld and becoming one with the animal. This is not the same as finding a totem or power beast – it is entering the deep, animal spirit and experiencing its essence. To an animal all has life, and the vividness and the 'beingness' of each stone and leaf are beyond anything encompassed by human senses. Animals do not reason or question – they simply do and are, they are totally identified with their purpose and the business of living. In many respects their life-force is brighter than ours. It is wonderful to experience nature without worrying about mud on your nose or wet

fur, and it is very empowering to our usual state of dull and robotic blindness.

Here is an example of a different type of Lowerworld journey. The purpose of this journey was to release creativity and to find a power source for a demanding project. The journeyer is afraid of spiders. This is what happened:

I descend through my tunnel on the drumbeat and I am in Lowerworld. The sun is shining, but I am taken down many tracks and byways, through undergrowth and stream-beds. Then I am admitted to a gothic-type mansion by a black-clad woman. I know there is something huge and dreadful at the top of the building, and find I am mounting the spiral stairs, riding on the drum, but part of me seeming to keep slipping down to the left of the stairs. I am not sure I want to progress …

At the top of the stairs is a large open doorway and I know that something horrific is beyond the doorway. I also know that it will not come out to get me, and that it is my choice whether I wish to confront it or not. I feel I must, yet I hesitate …

At length I come around the doorway and I see it. It is a huge, black spider, much larger than an elephant, and it is swaying forwards and backwards on the drumbeat. I am invited to enter but I really don't know if I can. I tell myself this isn't 'really' happening, but I am still afraid. My spine is chilled down its entire length, and I feel sick.

Eventually I do go in and all the skin on my body crawls and writhes. I go under the nauseating black belly and – horror of horrors – I am absorbed into it. Soon I am the spider. I stand there rocking backwards and forwards and, oh! I am aware of how hugely powerful I am. I need no-one. No-one's approval matters – I just am. There are no obstacles – I can do whatever I decide to do.

The roof lifts off and I grow wings. Flying, I soar over the trees and valleys. I alight in a forest by a large stone. Now I am human again and the spider is beside me – a little smaller but still huge. I am still afraid, my skin is still creeping. Another

spider emerges from the earth. I retreat, climbing up some steep rock, but I decide that I will come down, having come this far, and face whatever fate awaits me.

Now the second spider grabs me and pulls me apart, shoving all the bits of me into a big pot, under the shadow of the stone. It doesn't hurt, but it feels very odd and scary. I come out of the pot all moulded together again, but I am made of gold, and rather stiff. The spiders, who have now turned into beetles the size of large dogs and are no longer terrifying, grab hold of me and tweak me. I am no longer gold, no longer stiff. I am a savage, ecstatic woman with long black hair, and I dance like the wild west wind over the countryside, free, mad with joy ...

The drum calls me back and I return to my everyday self. I feel sick for an hour or so after the experience. I write down what has happened and watch some television, to unwind. In the coming days I feel a greater ability to concentrate. No major revelation takes place, yet I feel more relaxed and confident. But this is probably the beginning of something that will evolve in time.

LOWERWORLD PRACTICE – FAMILY MYTHS

This practice is really associated with the genogram practice, at the end of Chapter 1.

Most families have myths or stories that are often linked to the image of the family. Sometimes these may masquerade as positive traits, yet they can be very limiting to individuals who do not or cannot conform. This is rather more subtle and difficult than the case, for example, of a boy who is pushed to studying to be a doctor, because his father and grandfather were in medicine, despite the fact the boy shows artistic talent and wishes to go to art college. Family 'myths' can engender real fear and inhibit growth on the pretext of being part of something special, and the price of belonging may be loss of part of ourselves. To escape the myth may seem very disempowering at first. The loss of approval of relatives –

even if these relatives have passed on and are only voices heard inside our heads – can feel devastating.

Here is an example of the sort of myth and its possible results:

'Our family are clever, so no-one likes us that much.' (So if people like me, I'm stupid – I must live a lonely life.)

'They are all just jealous, dear.' (I can't trust anyone, because they envy me. I must never be envious myself.)

'We're just ordinary people.' (I can't be different, talented, extraordinary, rebellious.)

'You can say one thing for us Patersons – we're always generous. Meanness is a dreadful thing.' (I can't have boundaries, can't say 'no', must give away bits of myself and my possessions everywhere.)

'My sisters were all beautiful, like your grandmother, and her mother, too. We all had such happy marriages. Make sure you look after yourself, dear.' (Above all, I must look good. I can't have a career in engineering, can't get fat, look scruffy, slouch – and Oh, what will happen when I get old?)

'I was decorated in the Second World War, and your grandfather was a hero in the First. All this "sensitivity" stuff is an excuse for cowardice. No Harris has ever been a coward.' (I mustn't be scared of the classroom bully or ask for help. If I cry I'm a reject.)

'We're usually misunderstood in our family – that's why we haven't attained success. Your uncle really deserves the Nobel prize. Well, maybe one day they'll all wake up!' (If I communicate well, if I succeed, acquire acclaim, I'm selling out, and I'm just ordinary – otherwise they wouldn't understand me, would they?)

These are very simple examples, but it is not hard to see how they can create fear and pressure. Think about your own family. Does it have a 'myth'? You may need to think hard, for this type of myth is often accepted without question. If you do identify a myth ask yourself what effect this may have had upon you. Then you may like to begin healing the effects of this myth by setting up your medicine wheel and sitting in the corner of it that seems most appropriate.

For instance, if your family prized serious thought and discussion, and were rather condescending to anyone not terribly clever or well educated, your own spontaneity and emotional life may have been crippled, and you may find it hard to form close relationships – indeed you may fear them – because you need to intellectualise and dread being 'inferior' and childishly emotional. So, perhaps you need to sit in the South of the Lakota wheel, and meditate on all the associated ideas of innocence and childish trust. Perhaps you could think also of luxurious plant life, warmth, nude bathing in summer pools, red clothes, red flowers and anything similar. Later on you may like to journey on the theme of finding the South, to see what this may uncover. Within your fear of emotional vulnerability may lie the key to happiness and creative power.

Later still, when you have become used to journeying, you may wish to undertake a Lowerworld journey, to unravel the threads of these beliefs and their tripping, strangling effect. Occasionally, of course, a myth can be very empowering – which is exactly what true myth is intended for. Your self-questioning may show you how the myth operates for you.

Upperworld

This is the dreamed-about, sought-after realm, sung of by mystics and yearned for by all those who seek enlightenment. From Upperworld we can take all the petty things that disturb us in a panoramic glance that puts all immediately into its proper place and leaves us free to soar. This is the realm of gods and angels, home of the blessed, of all that is beautiful and transcendent.

This sounds wonderful, of course, but Upperworld has been subject to as much distortion as Lowerworld, called Heaven, and reserved only for those who have been 'good'. However, this section of the World Tree, its fruit-bearing branches, the place where we may hope to gather the harvest of our plantings, is nourished and is totally dependent for its existence on the Underworld roots.

As Lowerworld would have no meaning without Upperworld, so Upperworld would have no life without Lowerworld. This is forgotten by fundamentalist religions who equate the Underworld with a fall from grace. It is not always remembered by seekers of the 'New Age' on a quest for enlightenment that neglects source and shadow. However, no true access to Upperworld is achieved without acquaintance and appreciation of Lowerworld. Reclaiming the hidden powers of Lowerworld is the true meaning of 'redemption'.

In our journeys we can find inspiration in Upperworld and we can find the patterns and meanings that underpin our lives and form our spiritual quest. We may connect the realm of Upperworld to what we can call our Superconscious – that part of us that reaches above and beyond the ego, to seek connection with the Divine and eternal and true sisterhood and brotherhood with the rest of humanity, and the animals, plants, trees and stones that are our siblings also. Upperworld is about total visions, intuitions, guidance, progress and possibilities. When we can't quite 'see' how things will go, when we feel we are missing something, when we search for meaning and direction, Upperworld is the place we may go to for answers. However, the wisdom of Upperworld doesn't come without a sense of responsibility and balance.

Upperworld is the abode of the star-beings, of the planetary energies that infuse our lives, of the sun and moon and the gods and goddesses that are linked to them. Angels and bird deities live in Upperworld, along with goddesses such as Arianrhod of the Silver Wheel and Diana of the white and shining moon. Goddesses associated with spinning and weaving may be encountered here – and Arianrhod may be one such, along with Ariadne, Arachne and Athene. It is in Upperworld we may seek the thread of our incarnation, unravel it and follow its true path. Gods of light such as Lugh and Apollo may also be found here. The entrance to Upperworld is usually gained via some high place like a mountain or tree-top, and we shall be discussing this, too, in our 'Upperworld Practice'.

An Upperworld journey

The purpose of this journey was to discover more about the moon, her energies, message and relevance for us at the present time – in short, what we can and need to learn about her.

At first I cannot get off the ground – I keep bobbing back on to the surface of the moon-pearled lake, and all I can do is to watch her, brilliant Lady of the Night, from the ground. I begin to think this journey isn't going to 'happen'. I decide I will just enjoy the moonlight and wander around the side of the lake for a while.

Then I am airborne, but it is not as I expect, for I am whisked round immediately to the dark side of the moon and I realise it is this that I need to learn about. I see that the dark side glows with a strange, copper light, and there is a face there too. It forms clearly as the countenance of a fierce Aztec goddess – I have no idea of who she is. Her face is ugly, her mouth wide and grimacing. She seems to be telling me of all the suffering upon the world, seen by her bright face and stored in her memory.

She returns with me to earth, where she takes me on her gaunt shoulders and dances with me on her back. Dancing, dancing we come up the path to our lodge, and into the circle of all of us who are journeying there. Then she sets me down, back in my place in the circle and she dances. On and on, round and round, she dances, clockwise, round the medicine wheel. The candle flame casts her capering black shadow around the room, and as the drum beats she dances, dances, dances, never stopping.

I feel the Moon Goddess has told me that this is where she will be, that we have made a place for her, and although her energies are not always pleasant, as we may imagine them to be, yet there is great power in her – and she is with us. Her message for me is to bring things down to earth and to 'dance the dream alive'.

UPPERWORLD PRACTICE – STAR-PATTERN DANCING

For this, choose some music that really uplifts you, takes you out of yourself, sends you soaring. If you're likely to be embarrassed make sure you are alone, so you can be uninhibited. It is best to be alone in any case, unless you are with very like-minded people who are doing the same thing. You may dance also without music, and you may find that you are spontaneously humming a song, that seems to rise unbidden, within you.

Think about your birth sign. If you are familiar with your birth-sign constellation then you can dance out the actual positions of the stars – if not, just imagine them. (N.B. Due to a motion of the Earth on her axis, the precession of the equinoxes means the constellations no longer coincide with the zodiacal signs. This doesn't matter. Western astrology is based on the seasons of the year, and it is highly probable that the constellations were discerned and distinguished as a result of the earth energies prevalent at the time. In other words humans 'saw' a bull in the stars because a bull – i.e. Taurus – best symbolised energy patterns when the Sun was in that area of the sky.) Dance out your birth sign as delicately, as wildly, as quickly or as slowly as you like. Do this without music if you like, for ancient belief stated that each of the planets made music as it orbited, called the 'music of the spheres; and you may hear this with your inner ear. Do not think – just dance and enjoy. After you have finished you may like to write down some experiences, but the purpose is to begin to connect your consciousness with the stars and to be uplifted.

GENERAL PRACTICE

FINDING YOUR JOURNEY CENTRE

An important preparation to journeying is to find a place to start! It is possible to begin journeying without having established this point, and in time you will come to find that you have naturally 'found' your starting place, which you will use every time. However, it is much better to start as you mean to go on, and your journeys will be more vivid and meaningful if they are anchored in this way.

The journey centre is a place in the natural world – a real place that you visit often, or did often visit at one time. It doesn't matter if this place no longer exists in the same form on the material plane, as long as you can clearly visualise it. It should be a place with which you feel a special rapport, somewhere to which you are drawn. It should have an access to Lowerworld in the shape of a tunnel, hollow tree, stream that goes underground or similar. It should also have Upperworld access, such as a tall tree, steep hill or something of that nature.

If your chosen place still exists make a point of going there regularly, so that you learn every detail of the landscape and it is clear to your inner eye. When it rains, imagine how your special place looks, as the raindrops patter, colours are wiped back to green and silver and the earth smells of the opening soil. When night falls and the moon rises imagine the place changed to a magical land of shadow and strange light. Visit your place at these times if you can, so that you learn it thoroughly in all its moods and take an offering of seeds or herbs with you when you go.

If your special place no longer exists then you will have to use your imagination to recreate it. Go there, mentally, in peaceful moments – and then you are, in fact, undertaking a Middleworld journey. Look closely at every bush, stone and blade of grass until they are imprinted on your mind. Whether your place is still in existence in the here-and-now or whether it is now only in subtle reality, love it, know it and make it yours in a spirit of welcome and honour.

Your special journey centre should be a place in the natural world, in a garden, park, wasteland, woodland or countryside. It would be possible to journey from a city centre, using drains as a Lowerworld entrance and high-rises as access to Upperworld. I have not tried this and I don't know anyone who has – nor can I recommend it, for part of shamanic practice is to rediscover the healing oneness that has been fractured by urban life. However, we do not seek to destroy human artefacts or regard them as evil, for they have made the lives of many of us much more comfortable, and it is only when they are misused that they bring ills and troubles. Try this if you will, and see if it works for you, although I would greatly recommend a natural setting.

When you have established your journey centre you have done some valuable work. In a sense you have already begun to journey, for you are like a traveller who has located the train station or airport, and is now planning to embark on the journey proper.

5

TOTEM ANIMALS AND POWER ANIMALS

Teach me half the gladness
That thy brain must know
Such harmonious madness
From my lips would flow
The world should listen then, as I am listening now!

P.B. Shelley, *To A Skylark*

Then all of us in turn said, 'Mitakuye oyasin, all my relatives!'
That meant all two-legged ones, all four-legged ones, even those
with eight legs, or no legs at all. It meant those with wings and
those with fins, those with roots and leaves and everything alive,
all our relatives …'

Leonard Crow Dog, Sioux medicine man

The Meaning of Totems

A totem is a symbol, an outward sign indicating inner meanings of power and unity, and linking different levels of experience and existence. A totem is a living object, whereas other symbols may be inanimate. For instance, the five-point star, or pentagram, the circle and the triangle are all geometric shapes used by occultists. Cauldron, chalice and sword are all strongly symbolic within different traditions – likewise the cross, the Star of David, the crescent moon are evocative to people of different faiths. Symbols of all types are important because they evoke many things consciously and unconsciously, and one symbol could often fill a book of associations, art, poetry and religion.

A totem is similar, but it is more vivid, for it is both more primitive and more developed. Totems have a life of their own and they can be active principles that can take us with them on a voyage of exploration, while conveying messages to us about our place in the scheme of things. A tribal totem gives unity to the group of people who identify with it. Modern examples of this are heraldic figures, and such important emblems as the Irish shamrock. Expatriate Irish folk are often sent shamrocks by their relatives still living in Eire, to wear on St Patrick's Day, so they may still feel a part of the homeland.

For our purposes the most important totems are animal totems, for these help to connect us with our sources and to inspire and empower us – they are much more than symbols alone, for they have purpose and vitality of their own. An animal spirit is the essence of all animals of that type. It is widely accepted that we have links with the animal kingdom, and each of us has one or more animal totems that tell us something about our essence and purpose and where we belong. Animals are our bridge, our connection to our instinctual past, and this is honoured by indigenous peoples who show respect for the animals they kill to give them life. Animals can teach us the wisdom that they still carry and in many ways they are the first rung on the ladder that leads back to our deep inheritance before developing ego-consciousness separated us from primal oneness and wordless understanding of the universe.

All our relations

In the West we have wrought dreadful, heartbreaking destruction, misuse and exploitation upon the animal kingdom. Isolated in our bastions of intellect and egotism, we cannot see that by our actions in regard to animals, plants and the Earth Mother herself, we have disastrously undermined our own roots. We seek remedies for our ills, from depression to cancer, in ways that are often even more destructive. Stumbling blindly onwards we do not see that the way is to retrace our steps, to find the oneness we once shared with all of life and to reclaim our links with the animals, who are our true friends. This is not sentimentality, but a deep and proper respect, without which we can have no real self-respect.

Indigenous, hunter-gatherer peoples, where shamanism is still relatively potent, do kill animals, but they do so with respect, realising that they are depriving a creature of life, and that this is no small matter. So the animal is honoured, its spirit is thanked, and all of the carcass usefully employed. The animal dies in its natural habitat, often with little suffering – young animals are not killed, nor are pregnant females. Contrast this with the 'civilised' abattoir, stinking of blood and fear. There is very little that could be called common care for the creatures, let alone reverence for the sacred gifts that the carcasses are. Ancient cave paintings indicate the struggle humans have undergone to reconcile respect for life and the rupture of the life continuum necessary in hunting and killing for food – indeed this conceptual paradox could be said to underpin all religions. It is time – it is past time – when we must begin to reclaim our relationships with 'all our relations' before it is too late, for them and for us. Shamanic journeys are part of this reclamation.

Affinity with animals

Each of us has one or more totem animals. These may be animals with which we have long felt an affinity, and indeed if you have felt strongly drawn to an animal over a long period of time, and if that animal

70

seems to have appeared at significant times in your life then it is likely that animal is your totem. For example, if you often see owls before making important life changes, owl may well be one of your totems – there is a bit of you that is very 'owl' deep inside. Of course, some animals are more common than others – only you can know if that creature 'speaks' to you. However, totem and power animals appear on shamanic journeys, and it is true that we do not choose them – they choose us! Helpful animals can sometimes be a surprise, and it may be hard to welcome Mouse, or Turkey, when we always thought we had an affinity for Eagle! All animals are equal, and all have special skills, and that is something that is known to the shamanic seeker.

There is a totem animal linked to each of the signs of the zodiac – and these differ from the zodiacal animals – for instance, the totem for Taurus is Beaver. This totem links all Taureans and gives them access to something at the foundations of their being, but obviously this will be much more relevant to some Taureans than others. Totem animals are rather different from zodiacal signs, in that they speak of potential and offer experience, rather than being descriptive. In addition, there are totems for directions, as we have encountered in the chapter on the medicine wheel, and totems for each of the elements. The zodiacal signs fall into four directional categories, as we shall see later. So besides your birth totem there will be a totem linking you to all other signs of the same element – Earth, Fire, Air or Water – and a directional totem linking you to the two signs nearest you. For Beaver, for instance, there is also Turtle, totem of Earth, and Eagle, totem of the East.

There is an important point about birth totems, that will be of interest to readers in the Southern Hemisphere. Birth totems are related to the seasons, *not* the zodiacal signs. Thus, in Australia for instance, Crow, totem for Falling Leaves Time – the period following the Autumn Equinox – would be the totem for 21 March–19 April. So Crow in the Southern Hemisphere corresponds to Aries, not Libra – and so on. Naturally a totem animal that does not inhabit the part of the would where one lives can seem less relevant and motivating. In this respect there may be work to be done in finding totems that are apt for where we live, for shamanic ways are about feeling truly identified with the world about us.

The totem associations can be interesting and can get us started on our work with animal powers. It is very important at this time in the history of the Earth that we reclaim our kinship with animals, who are often very wise, simple and noble. However, a true relationship with a guardian animal is established only through journeying.

Power animals

A power animal is one that represents a special strength or purpose. A totem animal is a link, a friend. A power animal is a champion. An animal could be called a 'totem' because it is an important symbol, without ever having been encountered on a shamanic journey. In practice, however, totem and power animals may overlap, and the terms are sometimes used almost interchangeably. You and your animal will know quite well what the relationship is between you.

For instance you may commence journeying and find that you wait in vain for your usual animal helper. After a while another animal may turn up to accompany you, and it transpires that the qualities of this particular animal are just what you need for the journey. At other times your usual animal will come and travel with you, protecting and guiding. Many people find they 'acquire' different animals as they progress, and when that particular animal has 'come through' the energies in question are generally more available. For instance, if Bear 'comes through' we may find we are more able to protect ourselves in practical ways, also more meditative and wisely introspective. Those involved in shamanic exploration often like to surround themselves with pictures, figures, jewellery, relating to their special animal or animals, or with feathers, pieces of fur and such like. It is fine in this respect to have with us parts of animals that have died, and this is well-established shamanic practice. The Paviotso shaman, Joe Green, tells us:

> ... the otter came to me in my dreams. He told me to get his skin and to cut it into a strip about four inches wide down the length of the back from the head to the top of the tail and including the eyes and the ears. Then he told me to get two eagle tail feathers

… The otter told me to keep the skin and the eagle-feathers. He told me to use the skin and feathers when sickness is bad and hard to cure … When I doctored, the otter gave me my songs.

Obviously, it is not acceptable to kill an animal for a trophy, or in order to have access to its power on shamanic journeys. Certainly the power of animals will not come to us like that, and to do so would be to negate all that we believe and practise in present-day shamanic work. However, parts of animals may come to us, such as the wonderful owl-wing that Jan, our facilitator, retrieved from the corpse of an owl killed by a car. Appreciating the significance of such things is part of living with the sacred, the metaphoric and the multidimensional.

Tokens of our animals can enable us to feel their presence in times of need. If you have several power animals you may feel that you need one especially with you at certain times – so, when you need far-sightedness you might wear a ring or pendant showing an Eagle, when you need skills in tracking, teaching or 'smelling out' a situation you might wear Wolf. Generally perhaps you feel that Otter is your totem, so you keep a sign of Otter with you at most times.

The ancient Egyptians were well aware of the power of animals and their relevance for us, and so their goddesses and gods were often shown with animal heads – for instance the lion-headed goddess Sekhmet. Sekhmet had all the strength and prowess of a lion, and she was also bloodthirsty! Yet her human form shows that we can mediate these qualities in our daily lives, calling upon them when needed. In a situation where we need to be somewhat relentless, Sekhmet would be a powerful ally. Sometimes when going into a challenging situation it may help to imagine, just for a moment, that we have the head of the animal we need placed on our own shoulders, and that we look out through those fierce, wise eyes. Sometimes also it may be a help to dance our power animal, especially when we just return from a journey, for in this way we are dancing our animals out into the here-and-now.

It is possible to journey especially to experience the essence of an animal, and if we are fortunate we may be granted an intimate connection with the animal in question. However, that does not

make this particular animal either a power animal or a totem animal for us more generally. We are merely lucky that for that particular journey we were allowed so close, in order that we might learn and appreciate the value and purpose of the animal. We may emerge from that journey feeling that our eyes have been opened, although we know that particular animal is not especially for us in this incarnation.

Meeting totem and power animals

One of your first journeys may well be to meet your totem/power animal, and indeed that is to be recommended as the purpose of a first journey. Your animal guardian can accompany you when you journey, giving you advice, leading you by example and helping you to find your way down the paths of Otherworld. Sometimes your animal will go with you, sometimes you may 'become' the animal for a while, seeing and hearing with his or her ears and eyes. Your animal may speak with a human voice, or indicate by gesture, or you may just 'know' what your animal is trying to convey. You may meet your special animal helper by going to your journey centre and by asking your animal to come. Some animals are shyer than others, some come in unexpected ways. Any animal that comes should be asked 'Are you my helper?' If you feel sure the answer is 'Yes' cherish your animal for it is tremendously valuable and a great gift to be treated with respect. This is so, even if it turns out to be an animal that you don't much like, or regard as attractive or noble – which does often happen on journeys. So, if Tortoise or Weasel appears, and they are your helping animal, be prepared to learn from them, humbly! They are what you need, even if you might have preferred to meet Hawk or Mountain Lion.

Other spirit helpers

Of course, not all the helpers we meet will be animals. We may seek

spirit teachers in Upperworld or Middleworld, or ancestral spirits in Lowerworld. Some people have several teachers. Sometimes these are native Americans, sometimes they are Africans. Equally they may be people from other races, or from the past, or they may not be human but rather spirits of nature or goddess or god forms. Such teachers are wise ones from the Otherworld, who can help us on our journeys, especially when we have problems. In time, you will come to love and trust these teachers, and visiting them will be like a homecoming. You can explore and experience this for yourself as you develop shamanically.

Birth totems

We can begin to experience animal medicine by considering our birth totems. These are an intriguing alternative to zodiac signs and reveal other dimensions of power and personality that may be available to us. A few sentences of 'character sketch' for people born at the relevant times is included below. However, that does not mean that the energies of the animal totem in question are available only to those born at that time, and the descriptions are intended to be helpful to anyone who has had experience of, feels affinity with or has encountered the particular animal. In the end you will have to decide which totems are relevant for you, by journeying. However, birth totems are an interesting place to start. (Remember that readers in the Southern Hemisphere should refer to the season rather than the dates in each case – see page 71.)

FALCON – AWAKENING TIME – 21 MARCH–19 APRIL

The Falcon is a bird of prey. Riding on the winds the sharp-eyed Falcon scans the earth for all that moves – new ideas, fresh perspectives, broad panoramas. When he or she sees something worthwhile, downwards Falcon swoops, scooping up the prey and

flying off with it, back to the realms of cloud and sky. Falcon people are like this with concepts, taking the broad view, descending on what is worthwhile without apparent hesitation, but not staying long on the earth. Thus, sometimes Falcons do not stay to reap what they sow. They are impetuous, fiery and impatient. They are often visionary, idealistic and far-sighted. They need freedom, meaning and stimulation in their lives as they need air, and while they may have great effect on their surroundings theirs is rather the realm of spirit, of the sunrise that throws light over the land. Of course, Falcon people are found in all walks of life, but though they may cope with the humdrum they must not be chained by it, for if their spirits are not freed to soar they are sadly estranged from their birthright and may become very irrascible.

Falcons lay their eggs on ledges – they trust to the wind and sky, and although they are beautiful and can be gentle, they are not cosy and earth-bound. As a totem, Falcon can link us to possibilities, to courage, imagination and vision, freeing us from restraint and the inability to see the wood for the trees. With Falcon we may travel far indeed.

Other Awakening Time totems   Eagle and Hawk
Plant totem   Dandelion
Mineral totem   Opal
Affinity   Salmons and Owls
Balancing polarity   Crow
Element   Fire

BEAVER – GROWING TIME – 20 APRIL–20 MAY

Beavers are well known as workers and this is enshrined in popular metaphor by the phrase 'beavering away' at something. Beavers are wielders of power and with their sharp teeth and claws they are able to fashion their environment thoroughly to their requirements. In a Lowerworld journey specifically intended to experience Beaver, I was aware of the total identification of Beaver with the ability to do, control and act within his environment, of the joy of constant, constructive activity. Part of stone, mud and tree, taking them

through his nostrils and into his bones, Beaver identifies with his environment and becomes master of it.

Beaver people are practical, down to earth, pragmatic and productive. They are strongly linked with their five senses and they need to feel part of their environment and to feel in control. Often they are very creative people with something solid to show for their efforts and with a great ability to enjoy life and the pleasures of the senses. From Beaver we can learn the importance of getting our hands dirty and of engaging with life. Beaver can show us how to put plans into action, to finish what we start, to obtain a deep and glowing sense of achievement.

Other Growing Time totems   Eagle and Turtle
Plant totem   Clover
Mineral totem   Jasper Bloodstone
Affinity   Woodpeckers, Brown Bears and Geese
Balancing polarity   Snake
Element   Earth

ÔEER – FLOWERING TIME – 21 MAY–20 JUNE

Deer are swift and graceful, light of foot, skilled at camouflage and very sensitive. They can smell the approach of an enemy on the wind and are very alert. The smallest alteration in their environment is immediately picked up by their acute senses and assessed as being friendly or otherwise, and their movements to react to it are instantaneous. Even when still, deer seem tremulously poised for movement.

Deer people can be extremely subtle and sensitive to nuances. Their thought processes are lightning swift and they act on them with equal speed, so they may seem unpredictable and sometimes nervous. Often they are prepared to make a complete volte-face if it suits their purpose, for they are very adaptable, quick to understand, resourceful and communicative. Deer people have a gentle touch and subtlety, and Deer can show us the way to understanding and kindness. Deer

can see things from all sides, Deer is prepared to change – she is not stubborn. Deer is prepared to move and adapt, trusting her delicate senses to reveal the truth. As a totem Deer can show us the ways of instinct, trusting our ability to react quickly and appropriately without long deliberation. She also shows how a light touch can achieve more than a heavy hand, and how love and gentleness have untold powers. In Celtic myth the deer may represent the goddess, showing the way to the realm of Faerie, through the Hollow Hills.

Other Flowering Time totems   Eagle and Butterfly
Plant totem   Mullein
Mineral totem   Agate
Affinity   Crows and Otters
Balancing polarity   Owl
Element   Air

WOODPECKER – LONG DAYS TIME – 21 JUNE–21 JULY

Woodpecker's rhythmic drumming on the trunks of trees makes a sound like the drum of the shaman. These birds cling tenaciously to the wood of trees making nests with care and pecking away until the goal has been achieved. Woodpeckers sometimes drum just for the joy of it, as if they are 'getting off' on the beat of their own drumming.

People born at this time are similarly in tune with the rhythms of life. Security, home and family attachment are very important to these people and they do not readily relinquish that which they regard as theirs. However, they are also creatures of dreams and instinct, appreciating the tides of being that flow below daylight consciousness.

Woodpecker can show us how to build 'nests' – safe places for that which we hold dear. It can show us how to listen to the rhythms, both inner and outer, that control our lives, flowing with our energy tides, not against them, and listening to the heartbeat of the earth, beating in time with our own hearts. Woodpecker has strength of feeling and intuition and forms a link with nature, so we may learn to respect her truly, love her and enjoy her.

Other Long Days Time totems   Mouse and Frog
Plant totem   Wild Rose
Mineral totem   Rose Quartz
Affinity   Wolves, Snakes and Beavers
Balancing polarity   Goose
Element   Water

SALMON – RIPENING TIME – 22 JULY–21 AUGUST

The Salmon is a powerful fish, often growing to enormous lengths and showing incredible strength and determination as it swims upstream to its spawning grounds. To do this it finds its way from the sea back to the river where it was born, sometimes leaping high waterfalls in its quest. The Salmon appears frequently in Celtic myth, symbolising wisdom – this may be because it swims in a pool near the Nine Hazels of Wisdom, deriving its knowledge from the hazelnuts it swallows.

Ripening Time people are often quite regal, with a healthy sense of their own importance, needing to be the centre of attention and to develop a strong sense of their individuality and direction in life. They are far-sighted, able to fix upon a goal without needing to have every step mapped along the way and at their best they are wise, seeing meanings that others may miss.

Salmon can show us how to acquire true wisdom and a solid sense of self, shining with our own lights and finding our own direction. In so doing we do not have to ruffle the waters of others, but simply we find our own defined path, by the light of the soul.

Other Ripening Time totems   Mouse and Hawk
Plant totem   Raspberry
Mineral totem   Carnelian
Affinity   Falcons and Owls
Balancing polarity   Otter
Element   Fire

BROWN BEAR – HARVESTING TIME – 22 AUGUST–21 SEPTEMBER

Bears are strong, self-protective and resourceful, eating a wide variety of foods, living in dark places such as caves, and possessing enormous stamina. Bears hibernate, gestating their cubs in the seclusion and secrecy of winter, to bring them into the light when spring arrives.

Bear people are independent, preferring to rely on themselves and their own resourcefulness. Self-possessed and controlled, they prefer to arrange their environment according to their wishes. Artemis, the maiden goddess, has affinity with the Bear, for her name derives from the ancient word for bear, *arth* (likewise Arthur, the legendary king). Artemis is the goddess of the wild and untouched – she is not 'pure' but she is her own person, like the Bear. This goddess wrought merciless vengeance on any caught violating her privacy. Bears are gentle when left alone, but vicious when cornered. Mostly Bear people are quiet, methodical and gentle, but they can defend their territory if necessary and never relinquish their right to organise their own lives.

Bear is a strong protective force, bringing us common sense and a methodical approach. Bear can show us pathways into the mysteries of the land, and, because of its hibernatory habits, it is a guardian of the realms of sleep and dreams – hardly surprising that teddy bears are so often given to children! On shamanic journeys Bear is a powerful ally, making demands on us and telling it 'like it is' while looking after our interests fiercely.

Other Harvesting Time totems Mouse and Turtle
Plant totem Violet
Mineral totem Topaz
Affinity Geese and Beavers
Balancing polarity Wolf

CROW – FALLING LEAVES TIME – 22 SEPTEMBER–22 OCTOBER

Crows forage and scavenge for anything, from grain and fruits to insects and carrion. They are powerful birds, and there are many varieties, including raven and magpie. They tend to live in groups that make them seem almost human, and they appear at home on the ground as well as in the sky. Crows are adaptable and they bring balance, both in their scavenging habits and more symbolically, in that they look at the world first with one eye and then the other.

Crow people are extremely keen to keep the peace and maintain a sense of balance at all times. Crows do not like to be alone – all activity is best undertaken with a partner or friends. Crows get their way through charm. Although their emotional responses are often moderate, they are sympathetic and helpful. They do like to feel they can fly free if things get too steamy, but they usually return, to retrieve the status quo and create balance again. Often they cannot quickly make up their minds and tend to 'hover' between alternatives. Although Crow people are peaceable, sometimes a state of war is the only way to restore balance. The Crow was associated with the Irish goddess of war, the Morrigan.

Crow is a law-giver and a protector of secrets. The laws in this case are not human laws, but the laws of nature, and these encompass Otherworld laws, which may include the transformative shifts that we call magic. Crow does not always bring knowledge that one may wish to hear. Crow can lead you in the ways of mystery, and initiate you into the hidden and incommunicable.

Other Falling Leaves Time totems   Grizzly Bear and Butterfly
Plant totem   Ivy
Mineral totem   Azurite
Affinity   Otters and Deer
Balancing polarity   Falcon
Element   Air

SNAKE – FROST TIME – 23 OCTOBER–22 NOVEMBER

Snakes strongly represent the cycle of transformation through birth, sexuality, death and rebirth in the fact they shed their skins. Snakes slither and glide, appearing to move almost by supernatural means. It is well known that the bites of some snakes are lethal, and snakes seem to inhabit a primitive, instinctual world that we have almost left behind, and by which we feel threatened. The spiralling movements of snakes have ancient parallels with passage into or out of the visible world, and so they have associations with the great Mother Goddess of the Stone Age.

Snake people are often very wise, especially about the sort of things that many people prefer to avoid, such as death, sex and strong emotion. They have the power to renew themselves from a deep level, and often seem almost to inflict suffering upon themselves – the drive behind this is to acquire profound knowledge and mastery of self. Snake people can sometimes strike, when the need is there, but they are usually patient, accepting and deeply understanding.

The gifts of Snake are wisdom and healing – the cadeuceus, symbol of the healing profession, is a staff entwined by two snakes. Snake brings understanding, a sense of patience and timing, a profound identification with the instincts and the gift of transformation. Transformation always arises from a change in consciousness. The Snake is one of the animals associated with the Irish Celtic Triple Goddess, Bride (also known as Brighid, Brigantia, Brigit, Bridget) and in general has many links with female sexuality and wisdom.

Other Frost Time totems   Grizzly Bear and Frog
Plant totem   Thistle
Mineral totem   Amethyst
Affinity   Wolves and Woodpeckers
Balancing polarity   Beaver
Element   Water

OWL – LONG NIGHTS TIME – 23 NOVEMBER–21 DECEMBER

The owl is a bird that flies by night, roosting in hollow trees and barns. Its huge eyes see well in the dark, and it hunts for mice and other small creatures that scuttle on the ground. Owls fly soundlessly, but their ears are sharp. Their cat-like, almost cuddly faces conceal fierceness and almost uncanny abilities.

Owl people are often wise. Sometimes they seem just to 'know' things, for no special reason, and they are likely to act on their intuitions, wishing always to push back the boundaries of consciousness – and other boundaries too, for Owl people are expansive, positive and often optimistic. They are adventurous, and may be proud and self-righteous at times, but they are usually generous people.

Owl is well known as a bringer of wisdom, carried on the shoulder of the wise goddess, Athene. Owl is also associated with the Welsh goddess, Blodeuwedd, 'flower-face'. Blodeuwedd was fashioned by magic out of flowers, as a wife for Llew. However, the beautiful maiden was never asked whether she wished for the marriage, and she fell in love with another, and plotted Llew's death. She is then changed into an owl, which is interpreted as a punishment, and Llew is resurrected. However, as Llew may be seen as a representation of the dying and resurrecting Sun god, Blodeuwedd is thus instrumental in determining the cycle of the seasons, through the 'death' of winter and the life of summer, in the tradition of powerful goddesses – she is therefore linked to the total 'knowingness' of nature, and to the right of women to make their own choices.

Owl can give you deep insight and an instinct for perceiving what may be just below the surface. Owl is a powerful ally in those seeking to expand consciousness.

Other Long Nights Time totems   Grizzly Bear and Hawk
Plant totem   Mistletoe

Mineral totem Obsidian
Affinity Falcons and Salmons
Balancing polarity Deer
Element Fire

GOOSE – RENEWAL TIME – 22 DECEMBER–19 JANUARY

Geese are large birds that often seem to inhabit places that are lonely and windswept, such as moor and marsh. They can be determined to the point of aggression and are reputed to have saved Rome from invasion by their loud honking. They have been immortalised in folklore and were significant to the Celts.

Geese people are determined and practical – they are climbers and may be loners on their path to achieve. However, they are usually family orientated. Sometimes they are melancholy and may become depressed if they feel they have not come up to their own high standards. Although their feet are on the ground, their heads are often in the stars, and they can master the art of 'possible dreaming'. Goose brings renewal and achievement. It also signifies purification and unexpected blessings.

Other Renewal Time totems Buffalo and Turtle
Plant totem Bramble
Mineral totem Peridot
Affinity Beavers and Brown Bears
Balancing polarity Woodpecker
Element Earth

OTTER – CLEANSING TIME – 20 JANUARY–18 FEBRUARY

Otters are sleek, aquatic mammals, at home on the earth or in the water. Otters are playful, known for their sense of fun and apparent mimicry. They are loyal mates and caring parents.

Otter people are kind, humanitarian and adaptable. They do not always follow the crowd, for they are often unconventional, but they hate to be thought egotistical or selfish. Usually they are helpful and considerate, but they do not like to be tied down and may be unpredictable and capricious at times.

Otter brings joy and compassion, encouraging playfulness. Otter teaches us not to take ourselves and our concerns too seriously and to be pleased for other people when they achieve. Otter also teaches letting go, not in a spirit of sacrifice, but so that we may relax and take life as it comes, giving gifts and receiving also.

Other Cleansing Time totems   Buffalo and Butterfly
Plant totem   Fern
Mineral totem   Turquoise
Affinity   Deer and Crows
Balancing polarity   Salmon
Element   Air

WOLF – BLUSTERY WINDS TIME – 19 FEBRUARY–20 MARCH

Wolves have an amazing sense of smell and a great ability to track. They can sense danger from a considerable distance. They are strong animals, like dogs, and used to be prevalent in Europe, although there are now very few left. Far from the fearful creatures of Gothic myth, wolves are generally gentle, with a strong sense of pack and family.

Wolf people are sensitive and receptive. Their instincts are second to none when it comes to 'smelling out' friend from foe and which direction to take. They seek out hidden byways of mind and spirit and have a strong sense of their own territory – while their welcome is warm for those invited, they can be remote and withdrawn when they feel invaded. Wolf people have strong emotions and are usually aware of the need to protect themselves in that vulnerable area. Sometimes they may vacillate, wondering which 'trail' to take.

Wolf is a teacher and mentor and an excellent Otherworld guide, showing us how to be safe and secret in esoteric matters and to find

our way. Wolf shows us how to hunt for meanings. Wolf was important to the Celts and is sacred to the Moon, showing the pathways of the soul, by the inner light. The wolf is another animal associated with the goddess Bride.

Other Blustery Winds Time totems   Buffalo and Frog
Plant totem   Plantain
Mineral totem   Jade
Affinity   Woodpeckers and Snakes
Balancing polarity   Brown Bear
Element   Water

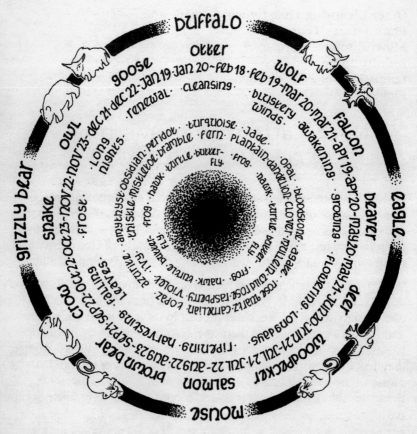

TOTEMS OF THE ELEMENTS AND DIRECTIONS

In our chapter on the medicine wheel we saw that the four directions had animal totems. When we plot the passage of the year on to the medicine wheel: Falcon, Beaver and Deer are in the East, and so their totem is also Eagle, the eastern totem; Woodpecker, Salmon and Brown Bear, in the South, have Mouse; Crow, Snake and Owl, in the West, have Grizzly Bear; and in the North, Goose, Otter and Wolf have Buffalo. In addition there are totems for the elements – Butterfly for the Air clan (Deer, Crow, Otter); Hawk for the Fire clan (Falcon, Salmon, Owl); Turtle for the Earth clan (Beaver, Brown Bear, Goose); and Frog for the Water clan (Woodpecker, Snake, Wolf). Let us now take a brief look at these animal totems, remembering they may have relevance to anyone.

Eagle

Eagle brings the light of the soul, for eagle flies close to the sun. Flashes of intuition, suddenly seeing the whole picture, climbing high spiritually – these are all gifts of Eagle. With his keen sight and speed, Eagle also has a magical quality and is frequently found in Celtic lore, considered to be one of the oldest animals and involved with the search for Mabon, the magical child. Eagle enables us to soar. Keeper of the East and the Sunrise, Eagle is of the realms of spirit and Fire.

Mouse

Mouse may seem a comedown after Eagle, but this is not so, for truly all animals are equal and have a gift to offer. Mouse looks closely at everything and sees what Eagle may miss. Mouse touches, sorts, assesses, scrutinises and as long as this isn't carried to extremes it is very valuable. Mouse can help us see danger or drawbacks. Keeper of the South and Noon, Mouse is of closeness and emotions and the element Water.

Grizzly Bear

Similar to Brown Bear, Grizzly is the largest, most powerful of the bears, knowing where to find healing roots and herbs and valuable things that are buried. Bear shows us where to search, internally, for our 'treasure'. Bear tells us when to withdraw, as he hibernates, to dream and meditate so we may reach our goals. Totem of the West and Evening, Grizzly is of the element Earth and the body and all the wordless wisdom this contains.

Buffalo

Buffalo provided the indigenous American people with all they needed, for food, clothing and shelter, and so was much revered. White Buffalo was often especially sacred, for it was a sign that prayers had been heard. The legend says that White Buffalo Woman brought the sacred pipe to the Lakota, and the pipe represents the union of male and female and connection with spirit. Buffalo brings a message of abundance, generosity and sharing and the wisdom that comes from being truly a part of our environment, not seeking to exploit it for gain. Buffalo is keeper of the North, of Midnight, of the element Air, and of the true mind, that seeks wisdom as opposed to mere knowledge.

Butterfly

Totem of the Air clan, Butterfly brings transformation, through its life stages, through egg, larva, chrysalis to brilliant-winged adult. Butterfly means freedom, living for the 'now' and willingness to change, as the winds carry us.

Frog

Totem of the Water clan, Frog is an amphibian, happy in more than one element. Frog can help us get used to change, making 'jumps' from one place to another, one idea to another, and impediments can be washed away in the healing, cleansing waters. Frog helps us to catch our breaths, jump back for a while to consider things from the viewpoint of what may be best for us and to wash away psychic negativity.

Turtle

Totem of the Earth clan, the Turtle was seen as representing the Earth Mother to native Americans, and America is called 'Turtle Island'. Turtle shows the need for groundedness and that the most important thing is to keep the body in balance first and foremost, before dashing around, physically and mentally, in search of bigger things. Turtle represents all that is healthy, sound and lovely in the Earth herself, and Turtle's shell not only signifies the rock that covers the Earth, but also perhaps the ozone layer and other protective attributes of the atmosphere. Turtle shows the way to our creative centre, and how to nurture ourselves and the Earth.

Hawk

Totem of the Fire clan, Hawk is the one who wakens us to true awareness, giving at once a panoramic vision and the call to look a little more closely. What have we missed? Hawk brings messages from the ether, from our unconscious minds, and prompts us to be on the lookout, both for problems and inspiration. Soaring high in the sunlight, Hawk brings a message to light the fires of our spirit and meet the initiation process of life. Some Celtic tales portray Hawk as wiser even than Eagle, and older than Salmon, so Hawk is a great ally on our inner quests.

Other animal helpers

Of course there are many, many animals that we may meet on shamanic journeying, or encounter symbolically in other ways. The following is a selection of just a few:

Hare

Long associated with the Goddess and the Otherworld, hares can be seen especially on nights of the full moon. The hare is associated with sacrifice, which means not masochism, but a search for the true self, which may mean denials along the way. It is not easy to identify

the nest of the Hare, and so young hares seem to appear from nowhere. Hares are not timid like rabbits and seem to have an uncanny quality. They were valued by the Celts. Hare shows us the way to the Otherworld, the mysteries of the Goddess and to knowledge that springs up as if from nowhere, in our minds.

RABBIT

In contrast to the hare, Rabbit is timid. Rabbit is concerned with facing fears and bringing them to the surface, out of the 'burrow' so they can be dealt with. Rabbits too show the way to the Otherworld, but their bobbing tails recede so fast there is no way of following them! With Rabbit we can turn our weaknesses into strengths, so we do not run away from sources of help because we are blinded by our fears.

HORSE

White horses are seen etched on several hillsides in the south of England. Horse can carry us to the Otherworld realms, if we will sink our hands into her mane and hold on tight – she knows the way. Horse energy is also energy of the Earth – the bounding, springing tide of Earth energy. Horse has much female, compassionate energy, and passes through gateways in all dimensions. The Horse is also associated with the Welsh Celtic goddess Rhiannon, Queen of the Underworld, and some say with sexual love. Rhiannon on her white horse is also Queen of Elfame, the people of the hollow hills. Epona is a similar Gaulish goddess.

BADGER

Badgers are similar to bears and may be aggressive when cornered. Badger shows us how to defend ourselves when necessary, have courage, stick to our guns when we must and to heal ourselves. Highlanders keep their money in badger-headed sporrans!

SQUIRREL

Squirrels prepare long and carefully for hibernation and are often quite daring, with a little encouragement, coming up to back doors

and outhouses in search of food. Squirrel teaches us to prepare ourselves for the future, not just by hoarding, but also by getting rid of that which might hold us back, on all levels, conceptual as well as physical.

SOW

Long sacred to the Celtic goddess Cerridwen, of the Cauldron of transformation and initiation, the Sow has an Underworld quality. Because she is very fertile, but also occasionally eats her farrow, Sow symbolises the trio of transformation – birth, sexuality and death – and shows the connection between womb and tomb – the mysterious pathway of resurrection and reincarnation. She is a powerful, initiatory animal to encounter and can inspire and change.

SWAN

Another creature associated with the Irish goddess, Bride, who was goddess of poetry, healing and smithcraft, Swan develops from the 'ugly duckling' into a creature of consummate grace and beauty. In Celtic tradition, poets wore a cloak of swan skin and feathers, so the poet could speak the language of birds, so this is an inspiring and creative helper. Swan teaches us to surrender to the flow of the universe and to accept ourselves for the wondrous creatures we are, without seeking specific change, yet embracing it when it arrives. Swan is also about transformation, and a helper in the process of initiation.

DOLPHIN

These beautiful aquatic mammals have become a focus for the environmental lobby, threatened as they are by the incursion of humans and pollution into the kingdom of the seas. Threat to the delicate balance of the seas may be the greatest environmental hazard we face, as J.E. Lovelock suggests, in *Gaia* (Oxford, 1991). Dolphin symbolises the breath of life, and the spirit of communication, which is rhythm, like the motion of the tides. Dolphin can form a link with the rhythms of nature and shows us how to achieve solutions in this time of crisis for the Earth – listen to Dolphin's message of joy and freedom!

Turkey

An animal best known as a celebratory dish, Turkey is a most valuable creature, meaning gifts, sustenance and virtue. Turkey may give you a gift – anything from a legacy to a rainbow – or it may mean you are the gift-giver. Either way you are blessed, and are part of the 'give-away' that we look at in Chapter 6.

Bat

Mysterious and sinister, Bat inhabits the darkness, hanging upside-down, flying silently in the shadows. With Bat we may face our deepest, darkest fears and be transformed by them. Like the Hanging Man in the Tarot, or Odin hanging upside-down on the World Tree, Bat speaks of the initiatory experience of the shaman. Bat can help us through endings, and deaths of parts of ourselves so that new faculties, fresh ways of life, may come to birth.

Fox

Fox is quick and wily, and he is a master of camouflage. Cunning and watchful he assesses situations, pouncing when the time is right and carrying off the plumpest chicken! Fox shows us how to remain unseen while we go about our business, waiting quietly for opportunities. Fox shows how we can become close to, and identified with, our environment, and learn thereby the ways of stealth – not in order to be sly, but so we may be effectual. The children's story, *Fantastic Mr Fox* by Roald Dahl shows us the best of fox 'medicine'.

Dog

Long known as 'man's best friend' dog has similarities to Wolf, for Dog also is a moon animal, sacred to the witch goddess, Hecate, and so associated with the dark moon time of metamorphosis, and secrets which must be guarded. The three-headed dog, Cerberus, was said to guard the gates of the Underworld, in Greek myth. Dogs are guardians of treasures, mysteries, babies, property, and they are faithful and loyal, often through gross mistreatment and neglect, for

they seem to have the inner gift of understanding and acceptance. Dog shows us where we need to maintain our loyalty and commitment, maining faithful to what is truly important to us in life and guarding our inner 'treasures'.

CAT

Another well-known domestic animal. Cat was sacred to the Egyptians, and some say the cat goddess, Bast, was the lunar (and thus more instinctual) face of the lion goddess, Sekhmet, who is associated with Fire and the sun. Cats are fierce guardians, and were used to keep safe Tibetan temples. Cats have been most unjustifiably associated with evil, and treated very cruelly, possibly because they represent the darker 'feminine' side of the personality (also repressed and maltreated), which is intuitive and sometimes wild. This side needs to be redeemed if we are to recover our personal power and wholeness ('holiness'). On this note it is encouraging that cats are the most popular household pet in Britain, at the time of writing. Cat can show us how to be in perfect harmony with our instincts and relaxed about ourselves – what could be more relaxed than a sleeping cat, whose limbs seem to drip somnolence! Cat shows us when to strike and when to sleep. Being a great hunter, Cat shows us how we may always be self-sufficient. Fierce and sensuous, devoted mother and fearsome predator, Cat shows many sides of 'feminine' energy and Goddess wisdom.

STAG

We have considered Deer as our Flowering Time animal, and of course Stag is very similar. The large antlers are symbolic of the Horned God, Cernunnos, Lord both of fertility and seasonal culling. Stag is an Otherworld animal, wise in the ways of the hidden. He is a powerful totem signifying fertility and the mysteries of nature.

The above is only a small selection, obviously. To explore further you may like to begin with some of the titles listed in 'Further Reading'.

PRACTICE

Of course, there is no better way to get to know an animal than by shamanic journeying, for if you are lucky enough really to become part of the animal identity for a while it will greatly increase your understanding of the creature and its gifts. If an animal is your helper or power animal, its message will also become clear. For now, here is an exercise to become part of the animal kingdom.

For this you may select a pet animal if you have one, or choose an animal in the wild. This is not a matter of 'communicating' with the animal, but rather of 'becoming' that animal, even if this can only be achieved fully for an instant – it is a true shamanic activity.

If you have chosen a pet animal you can take your time. Take up the same position as your pet, breathe with similar rhythm, imagine your heartbeat adjusting to that of the animal in question. Relinquish your own identity, move like the animal – become the animal, sniffing, growling, mewing, scratching.

If you choose a wild animal you will probably have less time and will not be able to prepare to the same extent, but your experience may be very vivid. As you see the white bobbing tail of a rabbit racing over the fields allow yourself to become that frightened, elusive creature for a moment – feel the speed of your heartbeat racing, your breath panting, your whiskers twitching. Now you head for the muddy warmth and security of your burrow – smell it, feel its musty darkness close over you. Or you may do this with any animal you see. It is not necessary to have a special affinity with an animal for this exercise.

Write down your experiences when you have finished for they may be fleeting and hard to recapture – you may not believe what you have felt.

6
TOOLS, CRAFTS AND PRACTICES

With my bird bone rattle and my goatskin drum
With my cold river eye and my hot fire tongue
I'm an unnamed star, I'm a ragged queen
I'm an untamed womb, I'm a jagged seam
You know that nothing is as it seems …

Carolyn Hillyer, 'Shaman-Ca' from the album
A Circle of Thirteen, Seventh Wave Music, 1995

The relevance of tools

There are several different ways of looking at the importance of equipment or creative crafts in association with shamanic work.

One can merely regard all tools and symbols as aids to the subconscious mind, bringing about transcendent experience and transformations in consciousness by association alone. So, for instance, the drum can be looked at as having no 'real' importance – it's just what the sound 'does' to the listener that counts. This approach can be appealing to modern minds, and it is certainly true that the effects of drumming and rattling, the ambience of candlelight are all very powerful when it comes to influencing our state of mind. However, I think to look upon shamanic equipment solely in this way is somehow to miss the point.

In the perspective of the shaman all things have multidimensional reality. We are surrounded by meanings, magic and metaphor. Drumskin has a voice, it has feeling and density – it has a back that we can ride on into the Otherworld. It retains some of the identity of the animal whose skin it comes from, it has some of the characteristics of the one who made it, and it also has a life and being of its own. Such tools have powers of their own, and to deny this is to lose humility and wonder in the face of creation and to cut ourselves off from much that is vivid and exciting, because we cannot comprehend it logically.

In addition, tools have a 'grounding' effect. They bring the sublime experience of the shaman back down to earth and root it in the concrete reality of bone and stone. It is of value to people who readily escape into the abstract to have something practical to do and to concern themselves with. For the more pragmatic, tools can be seen as an acceptable, familiar way to approach transcendence. Besides, reverential use of objects is an excellent way of honouring Mother Earth and own bodies.

So, if you are one to whom the shamanic experience comes easily, don't forget that the trappings can only enhance your experience and make it more relevant – and sometimes the truth of this is only proven in practice. Without actually calling my experiences 'shamanic journeys', I had been making them for years. Using tools has made them more powerful, and more down to earth. Besides, there is poetry and beauty in objects and rituals – so, with that in mind, let us look at a selection of basic shamanic equipment.

The drum

Perhaps the most well known of shamanic tools, the drum is closely associated with Otherworld journeys. The drum has been called the shaman's horse, and it is true that you 'ride' on the drumbeat when taking shamanic journeys. The rhythm pounds through your body and every cell responds, throbbing into life and awakening to other realities in a most physical way. I find the sensations given by the drum are strongly sexual and often lead to a very vivid trance experience, with a heightened sense of smell and sometimes touch. At its best this can be truly ecstatic. Uniting the rhythms of the human heartbeat with the pulsations of earth energy, the drum is a powerful, magical beast, to ride wild and free.

However, the drum is not a prerequisite for journeying, and it is quite possible to journey to music, or in silence. Indeed, some people prefer it. I have even heard it said that journeying on the drum can be extremely uncomfortable, as if you want to get out of your skin. If you are journeying on the drum then of course you are held to that rhythm and it may not be suitable, or you may need to change 'rhythm' in some way, but feel unable to. However, if you are new to journeying, do not let this put you off, for generally the drum is tremendously helpful. The exact frequency to trigger a shift in consciousness varies a little from person to person, and so you may need to experiment.

When journeying the drumbeat should not be listened to – rather it should carry you. If you find you are listening to it, try to let go of that and simply ride. The drum rhythms will at times be evident during the journey – for example, when moving or flying – but at other times not so at all, and you will probably forget about the drumbeat as such, if your journey is absorbing.

When the time of journeying is coming to a close, the rhythm of the drumbeat changes to that of the 'call back' signal, which will become familiar to you. This change in rhythm helps you to return to ordinary consciousness.

It is not always possible to experience live drumming, especially when working alone, so tapes are readily available. You can find

how to obtain these in the 'Further Reading' section. Drums for shamanic work are best obtained from a specialist supplier who loves and is in tune with the work. Drums can be – and often are – decorated with the symbols of the shaman's special power, or 'medicine'. Obviously this should not be done in a hurry, for it may take a while for meanings and purposes to become clear.

The rattle

Another well-known shamanic article, the rattle has a multidimensional voice that whispers down the tangled paths of Otherworld. It is the chatter of dryads, the skitter of dried leaves, the scamper of tiny feet in secret places. The rattle sends a shower of sparks into the ether, shivers down the spine, rainbow ripples through the aura. The rattle can set the scene, defining sacred space for shamanic work. You might like to rattle at each of the quarters on the medicine wheel, or sound the rattle to mark the start of shamanic experience. Kenneth Meadows writes 'Repeated shaking of the rattle is a signal to the consciousness to switch to an altered frequency. It can be used as a preliminary to drumming, with the drum in order to reinforce the drumbeat, or even as an alternative to the drum' (*Shamanic Experience* – see 'Further Reading').

The rattle can also be used in shamanic healing, diagnosing a complaint by noticing the alteration in the 'voice' as it is passed over the body.

It is noticeable that many toys that are given to babies are 'shamanic'. Babies are very close to the Otherworld and are reassured by such articles. In fact they make very good use of them, not merely in finding out about this world, but in maintaining contact with others. It is believed that while the fontanelle – the soft spot on the scalp where the bones have not yet joined – is still open, access to such realms is easier, and some channellers report that awakening this area of our brains is one of the tasks necessary in this developing age, heralding a breakthrough in human consciousness.

The candle

Candles are widely used in all manner of magical and religious ceremonies. They are intensely evocative of all that is both transformative and eternal. In our group the medicine wheel is set out on a circular mat in the middle of the floor and the lighting of the candle at the centre of the wheel affirms the presence of Spirit. After the lighting of the candle the medicine wheel is sacred space, and this is remembered also by the custom of always walking 'sunwise' (clockwise, in the Northern Hemisphere) around the wheel, once the candle is lit. Afterwards the candle is blown out by all in unison, directing the energies that have been accumulated to a suitable cause and making a statement of return to the 'here-and-now'.

Medicine bags, crane bags and power bundles

Many people on a shamanic path like to wear a small pouch around their necks filled with small objects held as sacred or special. These may be stones, feathers, crystals, twigs, herbs – anything that affirms the connection of the shaman to his or her powers and establishes a relationship with other levels of reality.

The pouch can be made from animal skin or from natural fabric, if you do not approve of the killing of animals. The pouch may be circular, with cord threaded around the edge and gathered up at the 'neck' or it could be a rectangle, sewn together on two sides. However, if you choose a rectangular shape make sure the opening is big enough to get your fingers through. There is a lot to be said for circular shapes in this respect, for they tend more towards sacred and balanced associations. It is simple to make your own and indeed this is to be recommended, for in this way the pouch is infused with your personal energy. Put in the pouch anything that reflects some special aspect of experience to you and wear it around your neck at suitable times, to connect you to the powers of the cosmos. This is your personal medicine bag.

A power bundle is really a larger version of the same, except these articles may be actively used – spread out on an altar, shaken in the case of a rattle and burnt in the case of herbs. A native shaman would be likely to carry healing herbs and other ceremonial objects in this way.

A crane bag is similar to a power bundle, but derives from Celtic myth about the sea god Mannanan, who seems to have been both a god and a hero, master of magic and an adept medicine man. He gave his name to the Isle of Man. His bag apparently contained such diverse items as 'the bones of Asal's swine', 'a girdle of the great whale's back' and Mannanan's own shirt. John Matthews writes '...the crane bag contains the shaman's tool-kit, with which she or he works as diviner, healer and walker between the worlds. As you proceed with your shamanic training you will undoubtedly acquire various empowered objects which have a special personal meaning, and these can be kept in your own crane bag' (*The Celtic Shaman* – see 'Further Reading'). The crane bag can be made in the same way as the medicine bag, but you will need a piece of hide or cloth about 30 to 35 cm in diameter, and you will need holes every 2.5 cm or so, through which you thread your cord, or leather thongs.

SMUDGING

This is a process of cleansing the aura and another way of defining sacred space, by the use of incense. The herbs used in smudging are generally sage for protection, cedar for cleansing, and sweetgrass for calling in the presence of Spirit. One, two or all of these herbs may be used together, and it is possible to buy smudge sticks especially for the purpose. However, you may also use loose herbs, and lavender is a good all-purpose herb to use as a substitute.

Smudge sticks burn without charcoal, and indeed loose herbs will ignite also this way, although they will need vigorous fanning to keep them going! People who find incense smoke has adverse effects on them may prefer to avoid charcoal.

The herbs or smudge stick can rest in a large heatproof bowl, or best of all a large seashell. Ideally the smudge should be fanned with feathers, or a feather fan. The symbolic associations of feathers are many, and we can think of the feathers as 'winging' us to another dimension. Any feathers can be used and there is a lot to be said for using feathers of native birds – but of course a bird should never be shot just for its feathers! The structure of feathers also resembles the fibres of the human aura – hence the expression 'My feathers are all ruffled!'.

In our group we take it in turns to 'smudge' each other, going round in a circle. The person being smudged stands with arms held horizontally at the sides and with feet slightly apart, forming a five–point star. The person smudging faces them and begins with the outstretched hand that is on their own left, saying 'Grandfather' and fanning the smoke towards the hand. Moving horizontally, still fanning, she arrives at the opposite hand and says 'Grandmother'. The movement is now towards the womb space and down the right-hand leg to the foot saying 'Creation'. Back then, to the womb-space and down to the other foot, saying 'Great Mystery'. The motion is then to the top of the head, and the smudge is wafted above the crown with the word 'Spirit' followed by the native American phrase 'Mitakuye oyasin' or its English equivalent 'All my relations' which means not only human relations and ancestors but all that lives, including stones and crystals.

Now the subject turns sunwise (clockwise, in the Northern Hemisphere) so they have their back to the smudger and the process is repeated exactly as before. Now the one who has been smudged smudges the next in turn, and so on. This is done earnestly, but also with giggles. The Sioux medicine man Leonard Crow Dog says of the preparations for his first sweat bath:

> My father and my uncle, as well as the few other relatives, put me at my ease by cracking jokes and making funny little remarks. Life is holiness and everyday humdrum, sadness and laughter, the mind and the belly all mixed together. The Great Spirit doesn't want us to sort them out neatly. He lets the white people do it, who have one way of behaving on Sunday in church and another for the rest of the week. We were doing something sacred, but this didn't mean we shouldn't laugh while we gathered wood for the fire.

These words are wonderful and very much to the point.

If you are working alone you may wish to smudge your sacred space by wafting incense around your medicine wheel. You may also pass the smoke through your own aura in a similar fashion at the front. Stand the incense on a table and let the smoke pass through your back – contortions are unnecessary and may be unwise! A cricked neck is a bad start to journeying!

Making an altar

When engaged on any spiritual path, an altar is a special focus and an aid to concentration and devotion. My friend Carolyn says that 'If you create a space and define it as sacred something will fill it – and it will be something good, something that is Love'. Creating an altar is a statement that you are bringing your spiritual truth out into the here-and-now.

For your altar you need only a cupboard top, or even a small shelf. The space you give to it will depend on how much is available. Naturally it is not wise to encroach on badly needed living space.

Consider also other family members. No altar can serve its purpose if it causes disagreement or derision. As a last resort keep a 'portable' altar in a box. Keep the contents simple, so you can set them out at a moment's notice. The box itself can serve as the altar, and you may set it up at any time you feel the need, as a prelude to journeying, for meditation or whatever.

Keep your altar simple. Clutter tends to detract from the sacred. Feel free to place upon it anything you feel is important – stones, feathers, crystals, shells, objects you have found or made, seeds, herbs, animal figures, a chalice or a vase of flowers. Choose a special picture or figure that means something to you to have as a central focus, and always have a candle, or candles. For instance, a simple altar could consist of:

- candle in candlestick
- central devotional picture (in frame) or statue

- small figure of power animal
- pine cone
- a stone you found in a special place.

Tend your altar regularly, for in this way you are keeping alight the sacred flame within you.

The sweat lodge

This is an ancient purification ritual from native America, but it is used by many people today as a ritual cleansing. It is similar to a sauna, but the purpose is to cleanse not merely the body but the mind and spirit. Kenneth Meadows (*Earth Medicine* – see 'Further Reading') describes it this way:

> *A sweat lodge is a temporary circular beehive-like structure constructed from branches of trees to form its framework and covered with blankets, rugs or skins. Participants sit naked around a fire pit in which the shaman places white-hot stones which have been baked in a bonfire, and pours cold water over them to produce steam and heat … the participants are not merely cleansed physically but purified emotionally, mentally and spiritually.*

The Sioux shaman Leonard Crow Dog describes the experience of his first sweat lodge (*Shamanic Voices* – see 'Further Reading'):

> *With his buffalo horn ladle, Good Lance poured ice-cold water over the red-glowing stones. There was a tremendous hiss as we were instantly enveloped in a cloud of searing white steam. It was so hot it came like a shock wave upon me … I dared not breathe … I just stuck my head between my knees. Good Lance prayed … He prayed for the earth, the animals, the plants. He prayed to Tunkshila, the Grandfather Spirit … 'This steam is the holy breath of the Universe. Hokshila, boy, you are in your mother's womb again. You are going to be reborn'.*

For those who undertake it, the sweat lodge is a cathartic experience that is a preparation for transcendent experience.

The give-away

This is another graceful concept deriving from native American tradition. The give-away has two aspects. One is letting go of what we no longer need, or what is harmful to us. This may include such things as disease, prejudice, envy, unhappiness and such like, which can be allowed to flow out into the cosmos and be transmuted. It may also encompass giving away things like clothes we no longer wear but are still serviceable, jewellery that may be of value but is not suitable to us, and generally recycling anything we don't need. The second aspect of the give-away means giving to others what they need, and sometimes this can mean letting go of something that we truly value, because we recognise that in some deep fashion, the thing no longer properly belongs to us.

In practising the give-away we are becoming part of the river of life, and we may hope that what is right for us will flow down and wash up on our shore – for that is where it belongs. We are realising that we are a part of something much greater, something eternal and beautiful, something that has our best interests at heart, and that we do not need to grasp, covet, yearn and hoard in order for all to have their share. So the give-away is an expression of trust in the universe.

Medicine shields

Making a medicine shield is an important way of grounding the experiences we have undergone and making a statement of our personal abilities and knowledge. The shield then acts as a decorative object and a reminder of what we are and may become. You may make a shield depicting your power animal, enshrining a special experience or representing elements of an important journey, or dream. For instance, when seeking healing for an emotional hurt, you may dream of a shining being leading you into a garden of herbs. In addition, to benefit from such a wonderful dream, you can mark the event by creating a shield of dried herbs, possibly representing your celestial guide by a picture cut out from a card, a

bright crystal or other symbolic representation. If you are someone who is not used to such craft activities this may be a hard task, but it is worth it, for you feel special each time you look at your shield.

Traditionally a shield is made from animal skin, but you may prefer to use canvas on an embroidery hoop, or felt. Card, or even the back of a cereal packet, can suffice. The circle is the usual shape, but I have seen diamond shapes and ovals – even a beautiful shield made out of a flat piece of crystal. It will be helpful if you can hang your shield on the wall in some way. You may draw on your shield, embroider it, stick things to it, hang beads, nuts or feathers from it – the list is endless. Do not worry if you feel you have no artistic talent – just play with ideas. Copydex glue is recommended by one of our group leaders, Jan, as being very effective and I have also found this to be good.

Your shield may be based on a theme, such as the experience of a particular journey – for instance, I have seen a shield based on the Yin/Yang design, created as a result of a journey to find out how to heal a relationship. It may be a statement of 'where you're at' or what you have to bring to a particular place or time. It may be a summing up of your life to date, a statement of your powers (such

powers are 'power to' certainly never 'power over') or a depiction of your intent. It may show power animals, symbols, photographs, spirit guides, moon phases – the choice is yours. Many shops sell a lovely range of beads, coloured stickers, stars, glitter, cord and feathers that will give you all you need. Like anything else, the worth of a shield can be appreciated only by doing it.

CONSECRATION

It is a good idea to consecrate any objects that you intend to use in your shamanic work, for in this way you are cleansing them of any less pleasant influences and affirming both to yourself and the cosmos that these things are to be used in a sacred manner.

Any consecration ritual should honour the powers of life and state your intention. The element Air can be present as incense, Fire as candle flame, Earth as a stone or bowl of soil and Water as a chalice or glass of water.

Ignite your candle and incense. Set up your medicine wheel and declare the space you are working to be sacred by saying:

'I ask for the presence and protection of Spirit in my undertakings' – or use words of your own choosing.

Place the object to be consecrated in the medicine wheel. You may like to place it in the centre, or choose the section of the wheel most suitable. For instance, if you had found a special crystal to place in your medicine pouch, affirming your ability to be still, inward and reflective you might like to place it in the West, if using the Lakota wheel.

Call in each of the quarters in your own words. Then use each of the elements in turn to cleanse. Pass the object close to the candle flame and say 'Be cleansed, by the power of Fire'. Likewise through incense smoke, water and soil for Air, Water and Earth respectively. Holding high your object say: 'May this … bring to me the power of Spirit and aid all my endeavours'. Add more words of your own, as appropriate, if you wish.

Finish your ritual by thanking the elemental powers for their help. You may then like to place your special article in moonlight, or leave it out in the sun, in wind or rain, depending on what it is and what you feel is appropriate. Moonlight is especially to be recommended, to 'charge up' important items. Then put it in the place it will henceforth inhabit.

Please note, it is best to devise your own rituals for such things, so feel free to do so when you are ready. Write down the ideas you have for use another time or to discuss with other people, to compare, refine and develop.

PRACTICE

This chapter has left you with several activities to attempt, if you so wish.

Certainly it is a good idea to set up an altar. Even if you cannot put into words exactly what you are enshrining, that does not matter. This is not a question of creeds – it is a question of feeling and searching. So put anything you feel uplifts you and draws you outwards and forwards on your spiritual quest upon your altar, regardless of how you feel this may look to anyone else. Making an altar is a good start on your path.

You may also like to go about acquiring some other equipment. Specialist suppliers sell smudge sticks and incense, and you will find a list at the back of this book.

You may also like to experiment with making a shield. You could start with something very basic that had a deep effect on you – perhaps a walk in the sunset, during which you were thinking about the Earth Mother and how valuable and beautiful is the earth we tread. So you might make your shield on golden card, showing a sticker of the globe in the centre perhaps cupped by a protective chalice shape, which you could draw. Around the shield you might like to stick feathers, twigs or small nut-shells you picked up on the walk. Perhaps you could dry and press a few flowers to go around. As you work more ideas can come to you. Indulge your imagination and have fun!

7 PREPARING TO JOURNEY

On the beat of a drum I am journeying
On the wings of a bird o'er the sea
On the beat of a drum I am journeying
Travelling where my soul is free . . . .
I ran through a field of flowers
And danced around a silver tree
And an Eagle came to carry me
And my spirit feels so free . . .

Lyrics by Beryl Meadows from the shamanic musical work
Powers of Love, Shamanic Experience – The Album, Peridot, 1991

Ready to make the journey

If you have read through this book, working at the exercises, if you have given thought to what the way of the shaman means to you, and if you have also read some of the books listed in 'Further Reading', then there is little doubt that you are ready to embark on journeying, if that is what you wish.

However, shamanic training is traditionally an oral teaching. You may get all the information and guidance that you need from the leader of a good shamanic group, without ever picking up a book. More than this, the wordless hills, the stream that laughingly moves ever towards you and beyond, tree branches, mewling like newborn kittens in the wind, the pad of the fox, the call of the gull, the spring of the cat – all these are the true teachers of the shaman.

You may have been making 'journeys' for much of your life, without realising what they were, or the experience may seem totally new to you. Whatever the case may be, shamanic experience is completely natural – so natural that it hardly needs to be written about. And yet so much has been lost to our conscious minds that we have to work to find the old pathways. We need to learn to open our eyes – so simple, and yet we have forgotten where our inner eyes are, and the lids are stuck tight after our long sleep.

Journeying is like daydreaming, except that it is much more focused, and it is like night-time dreaming, except that it is conscious and we are able to direct our movements and make choices. Most important, the shamanic journey always has a purpose, and this needs to be defined before we embark.

Defining the purpose of the journey

Shamanism is an active pursuit – it is not passive, like mediumship, or even channelling. The shaman does not wait to be 'taken over' –

she goes herself in search of that which she, or another, needs. Of course, shamanism does have things in common with clairvoyance, mediumship and other such abilities, for all these are concerned with alternative levels of reality, but the uses and approach are different and the shaman has a clearly defined quest in mind for the journey.

As you progress with shamanic work there will be many, many questions for you to journey on. You may ask about relationships or creative work you are engaged in; you may ask about life problems, transitions and important decisions; you may journey to meet ancestors, guides, goddesses and gods; you may journey for healing. It is best not to seek yes/no type answers, for this sort of black-and-white attitude is one we tend to live by, but it has little place in Otherworld. There you may receive guidance and wisdom, the skill to make your own choices or a new perspective that makes them irrelevant, and you will receive inspiration for more journeys. It is the journey that counts, as you will discover for yourself. For your initial journey, however, your purpose should be very simple, such as a Middleworld journey, to meet your power animal. Make sure that you are clear in your mind concerning your purpose before you journey.

Setting the scene

If you are journeying alone it is best if you define your sacred space before you start. You will also need to acquire a drumming tape, unless you intend to journey in silence. I think a drumming tape is definitely to be recommended at first. Later on, as you become more experienced, you can decide what works best for you.

Defining your space as sacred can be a fairly complex ceremony, involving setting up your medicine wheel, lighting a candle and smudging. Or you may keep it simple by just facing each of the directions in turn, concentrating on their gifts and attributes and asking them to be present to aid you. Then meditate for a few minutes, set your tape, settle yourself and commence. Be sure to

have paper and pen handy to take note of your experiences when you return.

Some form of 'scene setting' is important. This isn't just a devotional matter, although that in itself is vital to our spiritual nourishment and sense of meaning. It is also important psychologically as a protective framework – something greater than ourselves to which we can entrust our safekeeping and an orienteering system when we are in unknown realms.

Letting go

Your sacred space has been marked out and your initial meditations are complete. The purpose of your journey is clear in your mind. You have ensured that you won't be disturbed for about an hour. The phone is off the hook, and pets and children are being cared for elsewhere. The room is as dark as possible – or you have a silk scarf over your eyes if you feel it is too light. You are warm and comfortable – you may get quite cold while journeying, so a blanket may be recommended. Pen and paper are to hand and you are ready to start your tape.

It is nicest to journey lying down, but many people like to sit cross-legged. It is up to you what position you choose. Your next task is to relax, and that isn't as easy as it sounds, for usually even when we think we are relaxed small threads and knots of tension remain in telltale spots. These tension spots will interfere with your journeying in some way, for they act as pathways to doubt and distractions.

There are many ways of relaxing physically, and one well-known method of approach is to tense each muscle in turn and then relax. However, relaxation is mostly an emotional and mental state which may then be translated to the body. As you prepare yourself for your journey allow a feeling of trust to envelope you. Feel warm, as if your body and limbs are gently dissolving in a sunlit pool. Feel the universal web supporting you like a hammock and let your entire weight rest upon it. Let a feeling of wellbeing spread through you, so

your entire body smiles. Now take several deep breaths. You may breathe in the rhythm suggested by Kenneth Meadows in *Shamanic Experience* (see 'Further Reading') counting 'In ... two ... three ... four. Hold ... two ... three ... four. Out ... two ... three ... four.' Pause ... two ... three ... four.' Do this several times, but make sure that at no time do you feel any discomfort or strain. This has the effect of slowing bodily rhythms. Best of all, if you repeat this it will soon become associated in your mind with deep relaxation, making the whole process easier.

You are comfortable, deeply relaxed and prepared. Let the quest begin!

ENTRY TO OTHERWORLD

Now you can start your tape, and as the drumming sounds, go to your journey centre, your special inward place that you have become well acquainted with in our practice session for Chapter 4. Hold your purpose in mind and simply see what unfolds. Try not to attempt to control what happens or intellectualise or analyse. Simply watch with your inner eye, listen with your inner ear and ride on the drumbeat. Later you can think about it all, now is simply the time to experience, to travel the Otherworld paths, burrows and skyways until your call-back signal sounds. Good journey!

SOME QUESTIONS AND PROBLEMS

'I CAN'T JOURNEY — NOTHING HAPPENS'

This isn't an uncommon experience by any means, especially when we start journeying. Fear may be a factor, and sometimes even those experienced in shamanic work find they achieve little or no journey

on occasions. Rest assured that you can journey. If you have ever daydreamed, you can journey. Don't try too hard, accept that not much is likely to happen, but keep on playing your drumming tape or going to your group venue. Carolyn, one of our group leaders, has commented that occasionally a journey may consist of only a single flash of perception, after which you may return immediately to the here-and-now – but those flashes can be very important. Continue to relax and do not worry – the experience will come in time.

Caitlin Matthews (*Singing the Soul Back Home*, see 'Further Reading') has this to say:

> *People who have good mental control find sourcing difficult, because they have to let go. Journeying is about releasing control, not dictating what you experience. Trick the 'watch-dog mind' by story, song or monotony. Experiment by spending at least three hours with no possible distractions: you can do this indoors at night by switching off the lights; you can go out into nature and sit perfectly still; you can stare at a brick wall. Record what happens when you do this.*

Devices to break down our usual ways of perceiving and thinking can be very helpful, and once the transition is made, the way is then clear for future attempts.

'Is journeying dangerous?'

It cannot be unequivocally stated that journeying is without any risks, for here we are pushing back the boundaries of perception. In itself that may be demanding enough, when experiences become intense. In addition all of us, to some degree – and some of us to a great degree – are influenced consciously or unconsciously by our cultural perspective, which includes dualistic perception of good and evil and much fear and prohibition regarding the process of personal, transcendent revelation. This cannot be dispelled immediately – indeed it is something we are likely still to be struggling with for generations. However 'liberated' you may feel please do not imagine you are completely free from this, for if you belong to a Judaeo-Christian culture this is most unlikely. This in itself can make certain

experiences frightening, for old forms can masquerade in new guises, to put us off.

Besides this, if you have any history of mental instability, or even if you have weighty issues carried over from childhood that have not yet been fully resolved, these are very likely to surface during your shamanic development. This is not to deter you, for traditionally shamanism has been linked to mental 'derangement' with the shamanic experience being a healing one. However, you may find some things very difficult and the intensity may surprise you. For instance, I saw one participant at a workshop convulsed by tears because of childhood feelings vividly recalled by a journey in connection with the South of the medicine wheel. Some disturbances may also be felt that are too deep for tears. Be aware of these possibilities, be prepared to work on yourself, through the pain if necessary; obtain the help of a good therapist or look for support to your group leaders, who should be able to offer this themselves or put you in touch with someone who can help; ensure you have a network of understanding friends who can offer support and give you good advice.

As we saw earlier, the shamanic path is not a 'New Age' diversion, and needs to be approached with respect. However, there is no need for anyone to be put off. We have to be ready to meet difficulties and challenges – how else may we progress? Ensure you are prepared if some struggle should prove necessary – this will be far outweighed by the rewards.

'I feel it's all just imagination'

Well – so what? What is imagination if not the greatest, most creative, wonderful gift possessed by humankind? Look around you at the walls and décor of your home. Think of the things you hold dear – perhaps your garden, a special painting, your relationships even – all these at some point existed 'only' in the imagination of you or another person. Imagination is the supreme creative force, the building block of the universe. Never, never disparage it.

Having said this, there are levels of significance, of depth, of clarity. Also when the conscious mind is interfering, sometimes in a subtle way,

things are more suspect. Start by respecting all you experience, without regarding it as gospel. If you are doubtful as to the integrity of a spirit or animal helper, challenge it, saying 'In the name of love, I ask you whether you are truly here to help and guide me?'. No genuine spirit or power animal will mind this in the least, and anything that isn't as it should be will dissolve and disappear. As time goes on it will become clear to you what comes from a true source and what is misleading.

'I find I listen to the drum rather than riding on it'

Try not to do this. Relax and go 'beyond' the beat that you are hearing with your ordinary ears. If this seems impossible, experiment with different rhythms, or try journeying without a drum.

'I find I get terribly distracted'

If you catch yourself thinking about the shopping or remembering you have to book the car in for a service or listing the menu for tomorrow's dinner party, don't kick yourself or get tense and impatient. This happens to all of us sometimes. Journey on through distractions, letting them fall like leaves in your wake. Keep doing this, keep forgiving yourself. Sometimes you can even journey on the distractions – walk down the supermarket aisles with your power animal and see what happens!

The author Jamie Sams has a little trick to still the witterings of the conscious mind. Place the tips of thumb and forefinger together, on both hands, and rub them gently round and round. It is hard to think of petty distractions while doing this.

'I did not understand my journey'

Sometimes you may be given a gift (symbol, precious stone, book,

garment ...) but might not have a clue what it means. Jan, one of our group leaders, has a definite answer for this – journey again!

Journey once more to find out the significance of what you were shown – and again, and again if necessary. This could turn out to be a fascinating quest.

Of course, you can also use dictionaries of symbols to help you interpret, but be very careful not to take anything on board that doesn't feel right. If it fits, you are likely to experience a shiver of recognition – if not, then it is probably not correct for you. Sometimes the meaning of what we are shown may be made clear in everyday life. Very often like-minded friends can be a great help. But remember, if all else fails, journey again!

'Ωy journey was fragmentary – none of it made sense'

This is quite common. Write down as much of what happened as you can, and possibly come back to it later. Often it turns out there were bits that made wonderful sense, in among the confusion.

'I came back before the call-back signal'

That really doesn't matter. Some journeys are longer than others, or maybe you are more suited to short journeys.

'I wasn't ready to come back when the call-back sounded'

If this happens regularly to you, you obviously need longer journeys, so extend your drumming tape, or get in the habit of journeying again, to complete matters.

'My journeys seem "funny" and different from other people's'

That doesn't matter at all – your journey is valid for you and everyone has their own ways of experiencing Otherworld. There isn't a right or wrong way.

'If I encounter something frightening/upsetting/disturbing what should I do?'

If you are a beginner, do not confront such things – turn back. Your animal helper or guide can help you with such matters, and as time goes by you will know what to do. However, there may be things that cannot and should not be dealt with, for an individual cannot sort out racial or global matters single-handedly. All we can do is our 'bit'. Leave anything you do not feel comfortable about facing.

'Sometimes I feel "spaced out" after journeying and have trouble getting back to ordinary consciousness'

The practice of writing down your journeys is part of the grounding process, to return to the here-and-now. If this isn't sufficient, stand and stretch, walk about purposefully placing your feet firmly on the ground, bend down and lay your palms flat on the ground, and have a cup of tea. If you do all this it should bring you back to earth.

'People think I'm crazy when I talk about my journeys'

Then don't! You can't expect those who have not embarked on an

esoteric path to have any understanding of what you are doing. In fact, it is likely that what you say disturbs them in some way, and so they may react all the more unfavourably. Talk of your experiences only to the like-minded souls. If you have chosen the way of the shaman then you need to accept that you will feel isolated at times, but this is outweighed by the many gifts.

'ƉOW CAN I FIND A SHAMANIC GROUP?'

Some are listed in 'Further Reading'. Most 'New Age' bookshops and centres will have notices posted about such groups, so go to the one nearest you and look. Don't commit yourself to anyone or anything until you feel sure, and comfortable with those running the group or course.

FINAL WORDS

We are all aware that things are not well in our world. We have lost our spirit; we have lost our songs. Our oceans are poisoned, our air is polluted, our soil is tired and sick. We have betrayed the trees and animals that are our friends. Mother Earth is shamed and angry. Over the last 2,000 years in the Western world, we have lost true sense of the Divine, buried it under the dry and heavy stones of creeds and dogmas, barred the way to it by barbed-wire fences of fear, made labyrinths with no centre out of the workings of our intellect. We need to wake up to the fact that the gods are here, among us. We need to remember that the Earth is Goddess – and recognise this in our open hearts.

The way of the shaman sees the Divine in all things and respects them. She talks her talk until it becomes a song. She dances the song until she dances her dreams, the dreams of the Earth Mother, into life. Shamanism, as we have said, is an active pursuit – unifying, joyful, ensouled by true remembering, empowered by the fires of Spirit, walking the walk of the sacred up and down the everyday paths.

These are some words of Brooke Medicine Eagle, a Sioux medicine woman:

> *Any of us can dream, but when you seek a vision, you do this not only for yourself but that the people may live, that life may be better for all of us ... the earth itself is in need of healing. And I feel that any way that I can help, that is my mission; to make it whole, to pay attention to that wholeness, not only in ourselves but also in relation to the earth ... to allow your heart, your feelings, your emotions to distribute your energy; to pull that energy from the earth, from the sky; to pull it down and distribute it from your heart, the very centre of your being – that is our purpose.*

In following shamanic ways we take on a sacred task, not only to heal ourselves as best we can, but to bring healing to the planet. This healing comes not only from recycling, reusing, conserving and protecting. It comes also from uniting the Divine with the everyday, seeing Wordsworth's 'splendour in the grass ... glory in the flower' beauty, truth and eternity in clod, twig, star and stream, and seeing this not with sentimental eyes, but those of the pragmatist. Bringing our rituals into life with joy, humour and reverence; finding not new meanings but old meanings resouled and reclad – this is our task, our quest. Not believing, but knowing, doing and being.

Talk your truth, walk your wisdom, dance your dreams into life. May your heart be full and your steps light upon the earth, and may you be part of the healing process that we all, and our beloved planet, are in need of so badly.

PRACTICE

Our final practice session involves embarking on shamanic journeying – putting into practice what you have learnt in these pages, especially in this final chapter. Prepare for your journey in the ways explained and do not expect too much at first. Also remember, the whole of life is a 'journey' and the shamanic perspective can reveal its meanings – wordlessly, vibrantly and beautifully. Enjoy!

fURThER READING AND RESOURCES

N.B. Please remember to enclose a stamped, self-addressed envelope when writing to any group or individual.

Nevill Drury, *The Elements of Shamanism*, Element, 1992.
A useful little book on the nature and history of shamanism, containing also the words of well-known contemporary shamans.

Mircea Eliade, *Shamanism – Archaic Techniques of Ecstasy*, Arkana, 1989.
The classic work for all those wanting to find out about the history of shamanism.

John Halifax, *Shamanic Voices*, Arkana, 1991.
Words of native shamans from many cultures, compiled by an anthropologist who has an evident love and respect for the deep meanings of the subject.

Ronald Hutton, *The Shamans of Siberia*, Isle of Avalon Press, 1993.
Factual and interesting about the shamanic traditions of Siberia.

Kathy Jones, *Spinning the Wheel of Ana*, Ariadne, 1994.
'A spiritual quest to find the British primal ancestors', this book contains many interesting myths and explores several versions of the medicine wheel.

Caitlin Matthews, *Singing the Soul Back Home*, Element, 1995.
A very useful book, that is both inspiring and extremely practical. Less 'scholarly' than many works by this author, it is accessible and contains quite a treasury of exercises and information for the contemporary seeker.

John Matthew, *The Celtic Shaman*, Element, 1991.
An inspiring work for those interested in using the Celtic approach.

Kenneth Meadows, *Earth Medicine*, 1989; *The Medicine Way*, 1990; *Shamanic Experience*, 1991; *Where Eagles Fly*, 1995; Element.
These books are a comprehensive introduction to the entire shamanic experience, relevant for those who seek in today's world. Kenneth has coined the word 'shamanics' for, in his words, 'applying the essence of universal shamanism to modern-day living ... A prime purpose of Shamanics is to bring all aspects of ourselves – body, mind, soul and spirit – into unison'. Kenneth's **Faculty of Shamanics** runs workshops and a one-year Foundation course. Information on this can be obtained from: **The Faculty of Shamanics**, PO Box 300, Potters Bar, Herts EN6 4LE.

Joseph Rael, *Beautiful Painted Arrow*, Element, 1992.
A truly humbling book, rather a struggle in places, showing how the native Americans are able to live metaphorically and intensely, continuously aware of multilevel reality. This little book really is essential reading, even if you don't follow it all at first.

Gabrielle Roth, *Maps to Ecstasy*, Mandala 1990.
The ways of a modern shaman transmitted through movement and dance. Interesting reading.

Jamie Sams, *The Thirteen Original Clan Mothers*, Harper, San Francisco, 1994.
Native American wisdom of the Feminine, this beautiful book deserves to be thoroughly worked through, meditated upon and journeyed upon.

Jamie Sams and David Carson, *Medicine Cards*, Bear & Co, 1988.
Animal cards, with explanatory book. These cards are wonderful as a divination system, or to get in touch with your own 'medicine' (which is more or less the same thing!). The book explains evocatively the animal meanings, while the cards, much simpler than Tarot, really 'sock it to you' as someone put it to me! They can be used to meditate, or to explore possible meanings of symbolic events and journey encounters. I have found them very helpful.

Sacred Hoop – UK quarterly magazine for shamanic ways. One year's subscription £12 UK, £17 Europe, £17 Overseas (surface), £20 air mail, at time of writing. 28 Cowl Street, Evesham, Worcs WR11 4PL, UK. Tel/fax: 01386 49680.

Tapes and music

Drumming tape – a tape of information and with drumming, to take you on a shamanic journey, by Kenneth Meadows.

Powers of Love – musical tape by Beryl Meadows, depicting the shamanic experience, available by mail order from: Peridot Publishing, 27 Old Gloucester Street, London WC1N 3XX. £10 each, incl. postage & packing, at time of writing.

Music inspired by our ancient past and pagan roots – Catalogue available from 7th Wave Music, PO Box 1, Totnes, Devon, TQ9 6UQ, UK.

Courses and workshops

Eagle's Wing Centre for Contemporary Shamanism, with Leo Rutherford. 58 Westbere Road, London NW2 3RU. Tel: 0171 435 8174. Courses, workshops, tapes and booklets.

Different Drum – 'Unearthing the Magic'. Regular groups and workshops run in Cheltenham, Gloucestershire. Tel: Carolyn, 01242 528363 or Jan, 01452 770469 for more information.

Dance of the Deer Foundation for Shamanic Studies, PO Box 699, Soquel, California 95073, USA.

Suppliers for smudge, etc

Starchild, The Courtyard, Glastonbury, Somerset, BA6 9DU, UK. Tel: 01458 834663; Fax: 01458 831109. Worldwide mail order. Catalogue available, which is also a booklet, containing information on herbs, £1.50.

The Sorcerer's Apprentice, 6–8 Burley Lodge Road, Leeds LS6 1QP, UK. Tel: 0113 245 1309. Send two 1st class stamps, or International Reply Coupons, for a list of products. Worldwide distribution.